THE BAY TREE™

Artisan Preserving

THE BAY TREE™
Artisan Preserving

A COMPLETE COLLECTION OF CLASSIC AND CONTEMPORARY IDEAS

Emma Macdonald

with Susanna Tee

NOURISH

EAT WELL, LIVE WELL

To all those out there who love to make a good pickle.

Artisan Preserving
Emma Macdonald

First published in the USA and Canada in 2014 by
Nourish, an imprint of Watkins Publishing Limited
PO Box 883
Oxford, OX1 9PL, UK

A member of Osprey Group

Osprey Publishing
PO Box 3985
New York, NY 10185-3985
Tel: (001) 212 753 4402
Email: info@ospreypublishing.com

Publisher: Grace Cheetham
Project Editor: Rebecca Woods
Editor: Becky Alexander
Design and Photographic Art Direction: Gail Jones
Commissioned photography: Toby Scott
Food Stylist: Susanna Tee
Prop Stylist: Lucy Harvey
Production: Uzma Taj

ISBN: 978-1-84899-195-8

10 9 8 7 6 5 4 3 2 1

Typeset in Filosofia and Frutiger
Color reproduction by PDQ, UK
Printed in China

Publisher's note
While every care has been taken in compiling the recipes for
this book, Watkins Publishing Limited, or any other persons who
have been involved in working on this publication, cannot accept
responsibility for any errors or omissions, inadvertent or not, that
may be found in the recipes or text, nor for any problems that
may arise as a result of preparing one of these recipes. If you are
pregnant or breastfeeding or have any special dietary requirements
or medical conditions, it is advisable to consult a medical
professional before following any of the recipes contained in this
book. Ill or elderly people, babies, young children and women who
are pregnant or breastfeeding should avoid recipes containing raw
meat or fish or uncooked eggs.

Notes on the recipes
Unless otherwise stated:
• Use cage-free eggs and poultry
• Use medium fruit and vegetables and large eggs
• Use fresh ingredients, including herbs and chilies
• Spoon measurements are level unless indicated otherwise
• 1 tsp. = 5ml 1 tbsp. = 15ml 1 cup = 240ml

Watkins Publishing Limited is supporting the Woodland Trust, the
UK's leading woodland conservation charity, by funding tree-planting
initiatives and woodland maintenance.

nourishbooks.com

Contents

Introduction

Preserving is a way of making sure that fresh foods can be kept for longer, making sure they do not go to waste. This was very important in years past when the vegetable plot outside the back door provided the food that you ate each day. Preserving was a way to keep food on the table in the winter months. Today, when food is grown in huge quantities and imported year-round and commercial preserves are easy to buy, there is less reason to make preserves, yet many of us still love to do it. There is something very special about making a batch of raspberry jam from fruit picked from the garden, or making something delicious from foraged blackberries and apples.

I was brought up in a family where we used to come home to jars of green tomato chutney gracing the table and it was very comforting to see a pantry full of homemade marmalades and other delicacies. Today, knowing where all your food has come from is a rarity. It has made me appreciate simply cooked vegetables and how to make the most of what you have. The freshness and flavor that goes with homemade is not something you can buy.

I have always found it therapeutic and enjoyable to find ways to use up fruits or vegetables through pickling and preserving. I now have my own children and they are always keen to get involved in chopping onions and making jams; it is quite a family affair when we are all in the kitchen! Chutney has not quite been given the thumbs up yet, but they love homemade raspberry jam, particularly in a jam tart.

If you tend a garden plot or have a vegetable patch, it does focus your mind on making an effort to use up your precious produce; a glut of tomatoes or zucchini can very quickly go to waste. We are fairly obsessed in my family with waste, so we preserve, where we can, any food that we grow and we have chickens who eat our leftovers. I do confess to having no tasty answers to using a huge cabbage glut though, which I think many of us picklers find challenging!

There are so many fruits and berries you can eat for free if you know where to look. Foraging from the trees and hedgerows during the summer and fall can be a great way to get out and be active. Children can learn about the seasons and what grows when, and it's a great way to spend time together as a family. Start with fruits that grow abundantly near you, as it will be inexpensive to experiment. Sloes in the fall steeped in a bottle of gin makes the most delicious sloe gin to be drunk on a cold winter's day. If buying produce, your local farmers' market or pick-your-own is the most affordable way to get a good deal on a large quantity of fruit, and you can pick the best of the bunch.

Whatever you decide to make, give yourself plenty of time. Get your jars prepared before you start to cook, since jellies and jams can set quite quickly and you want your jars ready to fill. Once you have tried a few recipes, you will get to understand what sets well and what doesn't. You can start to be inventive with your ingredients and work with what you have at hand. The pot is your oyster and anything goes. I love inventing and mulling over what goes with what; many of my recipes have become favorites over the years and it is great to think they are unique in their own way.

What is Preserving?

Storing food for a long time needs a little bit of science. There are lots of methods you can use, such as curing, salting, drying, and covering with a layer of fat, as well as cooking using sugar, vinegar, or alcohol. All these methods help to prevent your preserves from spoiling and to last as long as you want them to.

All raw foods contain enzymes that help to sustain life as well as breaking them down, causing food to discolor and rot over time. Preserving halts the enzymes developing any further, keeping the food at its best. Preserving also works by drying up or killing off micro-organisms (for example, molds, yeasts and bacteria) that might enter your preserves and spoil your hard work. A high concentration of sugar, vinegar or alcohol, along with cooking at a high temperature, will prevent the growth of micro-organisms.

Mold is not actually harmful to eat but it tastes and looks unpleasant, and can indicate that bacteria are present. Bacteria are harmful as they can cause food poisoning. Yeasts cause foods to ferment, which is not wanted in your jam but can be a good thing in cider and breadmaking. In jams or other preserves, fermenting could mean that unwanted bacteria are present. Hygiene plays an important part in keeping your preserves bacteria-free, which is why sterilizing your jars and lids is so important (see page 14). There are many ways to preserve fruit and vegetables as well as meat and fish:

Jams
A combination of fruit and sugar cooked until they set to a soft, spreading consistency. The fruits used must contain pectin (see page 15–16), which helps them to set. If the fruit is low in pectin, such as strawberries, it can be combined with a fruit high in pectin, such as lemon, to help the jam to set.

Conserves
Similar to jams but are usually a soft set. The best fruits to use are soft fruits such as strawberries and raspberries; these are usually left in sugar for 24 hours to extract their juice before cooking for a short time. Some conserves, such as mincemeats, are made with dried fruits.

Marmalades
Again, similar to jams but are made from citrus fruits, peel and sugar. The peel must be cooked for a long time so that it softens before the sugar is added.

Jellies
Made from the juice of fruit, which is allowed to drip, then the sugar is added and the jelly cooked until set. Jellies can be served in the same way as jam but they are most often served with meat, poultry and cheese.

Curds
Made from fruit juice, sugar and eggs. Eggs are added to thicken the mixture to a rich, soft spreading consistency. Curds are considered a preserve since, traditionally, they were made when there was a glut of fruit, but they are not preserves in the true sense as they will keep only for a few weeks in a refrigerator.

Butters
Made from fruits and sugar that are cooked slowly for a long time until their consistency resembles soft butter.

They are used in a similar way to jam but do not keep as long, so should only be made in small quantities.

Cheeses

Similar to butters but are very thick and can be sealed in jars or small molds and turned out to serve with cold meat and cheeses. They keep much longer than butters and improve with storage.

Fruits in alcohol

Many fruits lend themselves to this preservation method, particularly fruits with pits such as cherries and apricots. Like vinegar, alcohol prevents the growth of bacteria. These preserves, like conserves, are delicious served as a dessert or with cheese. Whole fruits, such as clementines (see page 100), can also be conserved in sugar syrup.

Chutneys

A vinegar preserve made from one or a mixture of vegetables and fruit. Chutneys are cooked for a long time in vinegar, sugar, spices and salt until the mixture is reduced to a pulp, the consistency of a thick sauce. Chutneys need to mature since they improve with time.

Relishes

Similar to chutneys and the two are often confused. To clear up the confusion, relish contains more clearly defined vegetables and fruits since they are chopped into larger pieces, and the mixture is cooked for less time. Relish recipes often focus on one key ingredient.

Pickles

Preserve whole or sliced vegetables or fruits by cooking in spiced, sweetened vinegar. They may also be salted before being cooked.

Sauces

Blended or pureed preserves, made in a similar way, and with similar ingredients, to vinegar preserves, not dissimilar to chutney mixtures. Usually made from one predominant fruit or vegetable. They are pureed after cooking so that they are smooth, such as the popular tomato ketchup.

Candying

A sugar preserve method that works by soaking fruits in sugar syrup so that they are saturated with sugar. Candied fruit is then coated in sugar and left to dry.

Curing

A method of preserving meat, fish, vegetables and nuts using salt and drying. Salting draws out the water from the enzymes, which stops their growth and prevents the food going rancid. Drying closes the pores on the surface of the food so that it doesn't become exposed to air and harmful micro-organisms. Many cured foods are then smoked, which doesn't actually preserve the food but flavors or cooks it.

Drying

Used to preserve herbs, and some fruits and vegetables, drying works well for apples, pears, plums, chilies, onions and mushrooms. If this method of preserving interests you, you may wish to buy an electric food dehydrator to speed up the process.

Under fat

A method of preserving meat, fish and cheese under a layer of fat to seal it from the air, moisture and micro-organisms. These are short-term preserves and need to be stored in the refrigerator.

Ingredients

Choosing the best fruits and vegetables and the correct sugar and vinegar for your recipe will ensure you get the results you want. Finding excellent fresh produce has never been easier. You can forage, grow your own, shop at farm stores and farmers' markets, visit pick-your-own and swap home-grown produce at food swaps. Preserve-making is so popular that you can find unusual sugars and vinegars and other ingredients in most supermarkets, and readily online. It is easy to get started!

Choosing fruits and vegetables

Aim to preserve fruits and vegetables when they are at their peak. This can vary according to the weather and you can find your preserve-making time varies each year. You may find that if it has been a very dry year, you may need to add more liquid to your recipe, and vice versa. Your produce should be ripe but not overripe as it may contain more water than you expect, which may prevent the preserve from setting.

Many fruits freeze well, which means you can buy or harvest produce at its best and make your preserves when convenient to you. Seville oranges are perfect for freezing, which saves you having to make a whole year's supply of marmalade all at once. Choose large, heavy citrus fruits for marmalades as they are the juiciest. Some fruits, such as sloes, benefit from freezing. The best fruits and vegetables to freeze are those with a low water content or a hard skin, such as citrus fruit and apples. Strawberries and raspberries do not freeze well, but can still be used to make delicious preserves; a perfect way to use a bumper crop. A little of the pectin in the fruit is lost during freezing but this can be solved by adding an additional 10 percent of fruit to the quantity stated in the recipe.

When preparing your produce, discard any bruised or damaged parts as this will affect the quality and flavor of your preserve.

Alcohol

To act as a preservative, the alcohol that you use must be 80 percent proof to inhibit the growth of micro-organisms. Liquors such as brandy, gin, kirsch, rum and whiskies like Scotch are all suitable. Wines, fortified wines and hard cider can also be used but they must be combined with sugar, or heat-treated, to work.

Fat

Butter, goose fat and duck fat are the traditional fats used to seal out oxygen from preserves and so prevent micro-organisms entering. A fine layer of clarified fat is often used to cover pâtés and terrines. Oils are used too, particularly for preserving Mediterranean vegetables and cheeses, such as goat cheese. As the flavor of oil will impact on the preserve, use extra virgin olive oil; if you have any left in the jar after eating, the flavored oil will make a delicious salad dressing or you can use it to drizzle over broiled meat or fish.

Salt

Another important ingredient in preserves, salt inhibits the growth of micro-organisms. Ordinary cooking salt is suitable to use, especially as it is often needed in large quantities. Avoid table salt as this often contains anti-caking agents. For seasoning, you may prefer to use a sea salt, which can add its own distinctive flavor.

Spices and flavorings

If you make a lot of preserves you will soon have quite a collection of spices. They are important to give the final preserve its flavor and can be used whole or ground. Whole spices can be tied in a square of cheesecloth and removed from the preserves after cooking if you don't want them in the finished preserve. Ground spices are useful for chutneys and relishes since they make a clear preserve cloudy. Pickling spices are often used to flavor the vinegar in pickles, and blends can be bought ready-prepared. They vary in flavor so read the ingredients list. If you would like to make your own, see page 137.

Sugar

White granulated sugar is suitable for most preserves. Unrefined sugar, superfine sugar, sugar lumps, Demerara, and light and dark brown sugars can also be used but are more expensive; they are useful if you want to achieve a certain flavor or color. Preserving sugar is more expensive than granulated and is not necessary but it does reduce the amount of scum that develops during cooking. Jelly sugar contains added pectin and should be used with fruits that are low in pectin, such as strawberries. Most recipes will still require a mixture of jelly sugar and granulated sugar so the set is not too firm. Powdered sugar is not suitable for use in preserving.

Vinegar

The color, flavor and acetic acid content of vinegars varies widely so aim to use the correct one for each recipe. The acetic acid content should be at least 5 percent for preserve-making, so that micro-organisms can't survive. Vinegar color is no indication of its acid content so you need to read the label.

British malt vinegar is made from fermented barley and the dark variety is colored by added caramel. White malt vinegar has been distilled and is a good choice for light-colored pickles. It is sometimes described on the label as distilled white vinegar or distilled malt vinegar.

Red and white wine vinegars come from grapes and have a more delicate flavor than malt vinegar, as does cider vinegar, which is sweeter. Cider vinegar goes particularly well with apple chutneys. Balsamic vinegar is expensive by comparison to other vinegars but adds a distinct, delicious flavor along with its rich, dark color. Sherry vinegar can also be very useful for color and flavor. The vinegar used for pickles is usually spiced and you can either buy it or make your own.

Spiced vinegar

Pour 4 cups distilled white wine or white wine vinegar into a pot and add your choice of spices (see page 137). Slowly bring to a boil but do not allow it to bubble. Pour it into a bowl or bottles, cover and let infuse 2 hours. Strain the mixture before use.

Alternatively, you can add the spices to the vinegar without heating and let it infuse 1 to 2 months to intensify the flavor. Pour into clean, dry bottles and seal with airtight, vinegar-proof lids. Label and store in a cool, dry, dark place.

Equipment

I am not a great one for adding equipment to my kitchen cupboard, and you can make a lot of the recipes in this book without lots of special equipment. If you have a decent heavy pot, you can get going, and improvise along the way. If you want to make lots of preserves, one or two purchases will make your life easier. A candy or jelly thermometer is probably the most useful implement to buy as it can help you to find setting points accurately.

Bowl

You will need at least one large bowl for straining the liquid for a jelly and for brining vegetables for pickles. A selection of smaller-sized bowls are useful for holding your prepared ingredients.

Candy thermometer

This is very useful for finding an accurate setting point for your jams and jellies and it ensures that they reach the correct temperature to destroy any harmful bacteria. If you don't have one, you can still test a preserve's setting point by following the Wrinkle or Sheet Test (see page 21).

Cheesecloth

Small squares of cheesecloth are needed for tying seeds and spices in when making marmalade or flavoring pickles. You can buy small muslin or cheesecloth bags for this purpose, too. You can improvise by using a Handiwipe or gauze. The seeds and spices are then easy to remove after cooking.

Cutting board

You will need a large cutting board for preparing fruit and vegetables. I particularly like flexible cutting mats as you can lift the prepared food and scoop it straight into the preserving pan. They are lightweight and dishwasher-safe, too, for easy, effective cleaning.

Funnel

Useful for filling jars to prevent the preserve from spilling down the sides of the jar. You need to sterilize it each time you use it. Alternatively, you can use a large heatproof measuring cup to pour preserves into the jars.

Jars and bottles

Use jars and bottles with either a screw-top lid or wide-necked jars with glass or metal lids, secured by clips. They don't have to be new but it is essential that they are sterilized before use. I would, however, recommend that you use new lids and rubber rings, as secondhand ones could be damaged and could result in a poor seal. Lids can be bought in packs of various sizes from kitchen stores and online supplier. If the preserve contains a high percentage of vinegar, then you will need to use a vinegar-proof lid, which is lined with white plastic, or you can use a hermetic jar with a rubber seal. Hermetic jars are useful for canning larger fruits since they have a wide neck.

Jelly bag

This is used to strain the pulp into a bowl when making jellies. It has handles, which can be suspended from an upturned stool or chair. If you don't have one, you can improvise by using a double thickness of material, such as a lint-free dish towel or a piece of cheesecloth.

Knife

A large, sharp knife is an essential piece of equipment for preparing the fruit and vegetables. Sharpen it regularly.

Lemon squeezer

An essential, inexpensive piece of equipment for many marmalade and jam recipes.

Measuring cup, spoons and kitchen scale

Measuring your ingredients accurately is important when making preserves so these are the few essential items that you should buy if you haven't got them.

Preserving pan

A preserving pan is designed for making preserves since it can hold a large quantity of ingredients so your preserve can boil rapidly without it boiling over; it has a thick, heavy bottom so your preserve won't stick to the bottom; graduated sides to ensure that any liquid evaporates quickly; and handles and a spout to make pouring easier.

If you already own a large steel pot you can get started, but make sure your ingredients only come halfway up the sides. You may need to cook smaller batches, and add longer simmering and boiling times since evaporation will be slower.

If you want to buy a preserving pan, choose stainless steel since it conducts the heat evenly and quickly. Aluminum also conducts the heat well and is less expensive but choose a heavy-gauged pan since lightweight pans can dent and bow. Copper and brass pans should not be used for making chutneys, relishes and pickles since the vinegar will react with the pan and taint the flavor of the preserve. You can use them for fruit preserves but make sure you remove the preserve quickly to prevent acid damage.

Strainer

Used to puree fruit or make a smooth sauce, this can be used as an alternative to a food processor, especially if you need to discard the seeds. Use a heatproof nylon strainer rather than a metal strainer since the acid in the fruit can react with the metal and discolor it.

Slotted spoon

This is useful for scooping pits out of a preserve, and skimming the scum off jams, jellies and marmalades.

Wooden spoon (long-handle)

Good for stirring hot preserves so that your hand doesn't get too close. Some metals spoons can discolor the preserves so wood is the sensible choice.

Special equipment

If you want to get really serious about preserving, you may want to invest in a digital PH meter which checks the acidity of your preserve, and a refractometer, which measures sugar concentration. Both can help you achieve exactly the set you want and help to determine the preserve's shelf life. This can help you maintain the same consistency in a product, particularly if you plan to sell your preserves.

Sterilizing Bottles & Jars

The importance of sterilizing cannot be emphasized enough; it is essential so that your preserves do not deteriorate during storage. Always sterilize an extra bottle or jar in case it is needed. Remove any labels if you are reusing bottles or jars, and wash all in very hot, soapy water. Then follow one of the following methods to sterilize your bottles or jars.

In the oven

Do not dry the washed bottles or jars but put them upright on a baking sheet, about 2 inches apart, and put in the oven. Turn on the heat to 350°F and once the oven has reached this temperature, leave the bottles or jars in the oven 20 minutes to ensure they are completely sterilized. Most preserves will be hot when they're canned so it makes sense to keep the bottles or jars in the oven until needed; reduce the temperature slightly. Wear protective oven mitts when handling the hot bottles and jars.

In a pot

Put the washed bottles or jars in a large pot, ensuring they do not touch each other. Fill the pot with enough water to cover the bottles or jars by 1 inch, slowly bring to a boil and boil 10 minutes. Carefully remove the bottles or jars from the pot and put on a baking sheet. Put in the oven at 350°F and leave in the oven 20 minutes until dry.

In the dishwasher

Put the washed bottles or jars in the dishwasher and then run the hottest cycle. If the bottles or jars need cleaning first, you will need to run the dishwasher twice. Fill the bottles or jars while they are still hot.

Sterilizing lids

Put the lids in a pot of water, bring to a boil and boil 10 minutes. Make sure they are dry before using to avoid condensation forming. An alternative method is to fill the hot sterilized bottles or jars with the hot preserve, screw on the lids and then turn the bottles or jars upside down 1 minute. Wear protective oven mitts or cover the bottle or jar with a kitchen towel when you do this to avoid burning yourself. This effectively sterilizes the insides of the lids.

Sterilizing equipment

It is important that all the cooking equipment you use is scrupulously clean, too, to prevent bacteria passing into your preserves. Like bottles and jars, make sure that all pans, bowls, measuring cups, funnels and utensils are washed in very hot, soapy water and rinsed well, or run through the hottest dishwasher cycle just before using, even if they were washed well last time you used them.

Emma's tip Use the jars while they are still hot so that they do not crack when filled with the hot preserve.

Making Sweet Preserves

Jams, jellies, marmalades, butters and cheeses are all made following the same basic tried-and-tested methods, which produce their correct setting consistency, and it is their high concentration of sugar that preserves them.

All sweet preserves need pectin and acid to make them set. Fruits rich in pectin are usually rich in acid, too. If a fruit or vegetable has a low content of pectin or acid, it can be combined with a fruit with a high content to help it set. Lemon juice is often used to add extra acid where needed. As a guide, add 2 tablespoons lemon juice for every 4½ pounds fruit. You can also buy liquid or powdered pectin to add, which does not add a particular flavor so is very versatile.

Sweet preserves need a lot of sugar; the exact amount depends on the pectin content of the fruit, so always use the amount given in the recipes. It might be tempting to add less, but it will result in a preserve that won't set and it will also not keep well.

All sweet preserves are made by preparing the fruit, adding water and simmering until it is soft and reduced. When you add the sugar and any extra pectin varies for each recipe.

The cooking time for each recipe will depend on how hard or soft the fruit is. Don't try to speed up the cooking process, as it is during this time that the natural pectin and acid in the fruit are released.

When making jellies, the fruit is cooked to a pulp and then allowed to drip through a jelly bag to extract the fruit's juices. Whether you use a traditional jelly bag or you improvise, your bag should be scalded in boiling water before you use it so that the juices drip through it and are not absorbed by the bag. It's very tempting to squeeze the bag or prod the pulp but try to resist as it will produce a cloudy jelly. The general rule for jellies is to add 1 cup sugar to every 1 cup of juice extract.

Butter and cheese preserves are made to have a firm set. The general rule is to add ¾ cup sugar to every 1 cup of puree when making a butter, and 1 cup sugar to every 1 cup of puree when making a cheese. The sugar is added to the fruit when it is soft and not before, because if added too early it hardens the fruit and any peel, and will not soften further during cooking.

The key to all sweet preserves is making sure the sugar dissolves properly before you boil. You can warm the sugar beforehand in the oven at a low temperature

---

How much sugar?

Fruit with a high natural pectin content needs more sugar than fruit with low pectin. As a rough guide this is the amount of sugar you will need:

- 2¼ pounds fruit with a high pectin content needs up to 6¼ cups granulated sugar

- 2¼ pounds fruit with a medium pectin content needs up to 5 cups granulated sugar

- 2¼ pounds fruit with a low pectin content needs about 4 cups granulated sugar

Fruit and vegetable pectin content

Natural pectin content does vary from year to year, and during the season, due to a fruit's quality and different environmental conditions. It is also higher just before ripening. To test the pectin content of a fruit, add 1 teaspoon cooked fruit juice to 1 tablespoon denatured alcohol, gin or Scotch. If it forms a firm clot, it is high in pectin; if it forms small clots, it is medium; and if it remains liquid, it is low in pectin.

High	Medium	Low
Apples (cooking)	Apples (eating)	Bananas
Black currants	Apricots	Blackberries
Crab apples	Bilberries	(late)
Cranberries	Blackberries	Blueberries
Damson plums	(early)	Carrots
Gooseberries	Greengage	Cherries
Grapefruits	Loganberries	Elderberries
Grapes	Mulberries	Figs
Japonicas	Raspberries	Marrows
Lemons	Sloes	Medlar
Limes		Melons
Oranges		Nectarines
Plums (most		Peaches
varieties)		Pears
Quinces		Pineapple
Red currants		Pumpkin
White currants		Rhubarb
		Rosehips
		Strawberries
		Zucchini

so it dissolves quickly when in the fruit. Do not stir too much during the boiling time as it can cool the preserve. The boiling time will vary depending on the fruit used.

When testing for a set, take the pot off the burner so that the preserve doesn't cook unnecessarily for too long. Setting point is usually 221°F (see page 21).

Some recipes ask you to remove "scum" from the surface of your sweet preserve; scum is the bubbles caused by rapid boiling and is removed to help with the final appearance of the preserve. Adding a little butter helps to remove the scum but it is not essential.

Preserves containing whole fruits or peel should be left to cool about 15 minutes before canning to prevent the fruit or peel from rising in the jars.

Candied and crystallized fruits

These are other sweet preserves that rely on sugar to preserve them but are made by a different method. They are made by steeping the fruits in a sugar syrup over a period of time so that they soak up the sugar to a high concentration. Crystallized fruits are candied fruits that are then finely coated in a layer of sugar.

Emma's tip The recipes give the quantities each preserve makes but, in the case of jellies, this is a guide only. It will depend on how ripe the fruit was and how long it was left to drip, as these factors affect how much juice is obtained.

Making Savory Preserves

Chutneys, relishes, pickles and sauces have been made for generations as a way to preserve precious fruits and vegetables, and because they taste delicious. The basic method stays the same and uses vinegar, salt and/or sugar as the preservative. Cooks have experimented over the years with different combinations of produce, and by adding dried fruits, spices, chilies and garlic, to add flavor and bring their savory preserves to life.

Chutneys and relishes are made in a very similar way; the main differences are the preparation of the fruit and vegetables and their cooking time, which affect their final appearance. The ingredients for a relish are usually chopped into small pieces, while those for chutney are more roughly chopped. Chutneys are cooked a long time, which reduces the fruits and vegetables to a thick, pulpy mixture, whereas relishes are cooked a shorter time and the result tends to be a chunkier texture.

Unlike jam-making, you can use very ripe fruits and vegetables for savory preserves but do remove any damaged or bruised pieces. It is worth spending time carefully preparing fruit and vegetables for a relish as your slicing skills will be visible in the final preserve. You need to cook chutneys and relishes very slowly in a preserving pan or large pot, stirring from time to time to prevent them from sticking to the bottom of the pan. This is especially important near the end of cooking. Use a stainless steel pan as the vinegar in the preserve will react with copper or brass pans.

Pickles are usually made from a single fruit or vegetable and can be raw or cooked. Your produce should be firm and fresh so that its texture and flavor keep during storage. Many pickles are salted or "brined" first, either by dry salting where they are layered in salt (produce such as cucumbers that contain a lot of water use this method), or by wet salting, where they are soaked in a solution of salt and water. This draws out moisture and helps to retain color and crispness. After brining, rinse well and pat dry; wet vegetables will dilute the vinegar and the pickle is more likely to turn moldy.

Pickle texture

Cold vinegar is added to make crisp pickles and hot vinegar is added to make soft pickles. Some pickles, such as piccalilli are cooked in a sauce but the key is to retain the shape and texture of each vegetable in the pickle. Packing your jars too tightly can bruise the pickle; make sure all the ingredients are submerged in the liquid.

Sauces, such as tomato ketchup, are pureed to give a smooth, pouring consistency. You can puree using a food processor or push the mixture through a nylon strainer to make it smooth (metal can taint a sauce's flavor).

Storage and maturing

All preserves that contain vinegar should be covered with a clip-top glass lid or lids that have a vinegar-proof lining; metal lids will rust in direct contact with vinegar. Almost all chutneys, relishes and pickles should be allowed to mature at least a month before eating as they really do improve with age, and they can be stored at least a year. Pickled cabbage is an exception; it can't be stored more than 3 weeks as it loses its crispness. Sauces are best eaten within 3 months or you can can them in a water bath to prolong their storage life (see page 23). You can also store them in the freezer.

Making Canned Fruits & Drinks

Canned fruits, in either syrup or alcohol, make delicious desserts, and it is an excellent way to preserve whole or sliced fruits. Freezing has tended to replace the need to can fruits, but a jar or two can be a treat and make attractive gifts.

Choose fresh, perfect-quality fruit for canning, since presentation is part of the appeal. Choose attractive bottles and jars with wide necks so you can get the fruit in easily. Take time arranging the fruit in the bottle or jar so that they look attractive. It is traditional, for example, to arrange slices around the outside. Use the handle of a wooden spoon to move the fruit into position and pack tightly but without squashing or damaging them; the fruit is then less likely to rise in the jar.

If you plan to use liqueur or a liquor to cover the fruit it must have at least 40 percent (80 proof) alcohol to act as a preservative. Test that the flavor is compatible with the fruit used. Brandy complements most fruits. Kirsch, of course, works with cherries, but it is also delicious with raspberries and pineapple. Wines, fortified wines, sherry and hard cider can be used to bottle fruit but need to be combined with sugar to act as a preservative.

Syrups

Homemade fruit syrups are full of flavor and have more adult appeal than many commercial soft drinks. Most fruit syrups are made from soft berry fruits, such as black currants, and they need to be just ripe. The juices are extracted from the fruit usually by being left to soak in water overnight, then strained, cooked with sugar the following day, and strained again before being bottled. Soft fruit drinks do not have a long storage life but, stored in plastic bottles, they can be kept in the freezer. Allow a head-space at the top of the bottles to allow for the liquid to expand.

Fruit liqueurs such as Limoncello (see page 120) are made by infusing a liquor with fruit, sometimes with the addition of sugar to sweeten, and left in a warm place for several months. The infused liquid is transferred into sterilized bottles and can keep for many years. If you like, the fruits can be served separately as an alcoholic dessert. Gin was traditionally flavored with sloes and damson plums, rum works very well with plums, and vodka and black currants are also a great match.

Mincemeats

Brandy, rum and sherry all work well in mincemeat. The dried fruits are preserved in both sugar and alcohol, and it is important that the fruits are well submerged.

Emma's tip The recipes indicate the size and number of jars that you need but when packing fruits in jars, it is difficult to be specific as it depends on the size of the fruits and how tightly you pack them. It is advisable to have an extra jar ready just in case it is needed.

Making Cured, Dried & Potted Preserves

Curing and drying works by removing moisture so micro-organisms cannot grow. Curing used to be a very popular way of preserving meat but is less often used now due to freezing. Traditional methods such as the British technique called potting remain popular as they enhance flavor and texture.

Cured preserves

Many people enjoy the flavor curing brings to food, and some meats can be dried in the home (see Cured Leg of Lamb on page 221) although it does need a lot of care. Many cured foods, such as salmon, are also smoked, which dries the food further and adds flavor. If you want to smoke food you can buy or make a smoker to give food a delicious smoky flavor, but it won't actually preserve it. For suggestions on the type of salt to use, see page 10. Very fresh, cold meat and fish should be used for curing, not frozen, as freezing makes food cells expand and absorb more salt than is needed.

Dried preserves

Drying fruits and vegetables is less complicated, although some foods are more suitable than others. Apples, apricots, pears, plums, onions, mushrooms and herbs can all be dried successfully in the home in a low oven. The temperature must be low enough to dry, rather than bake the food, as otherwise it will shrivel. Ventilation is needed and the longer the period over which the food is dried the better for success. You can buy domestic dehydrators, which can be useful if you have a large supply of produce to dry. Choose fresh, perfect-quality fruit and vegetables that are just ripe and don't have any bruises or blemishes. Once dried, it is important to store the food away from any moisture to preserve it, as the food may absorb water again and start to rehydrate.

Potted preserves

The British method of potting preserves foods under a seal of fat. This seal excludes moisture and air—and therefore any harmful micro-organisms—from getting into the foods. Potted foods, such as pâtés and terrines, are "short-term" preserves as they must be kept in the refrigerator and cannot be stored for a long time. Once the seal of fat is broken, the preserve should be eaten within a week. Like curing foods, meat or fish to be potted is usually layered with salt to remove as much moisture as possible, and then cooked for a long time until tender. The most suitable meats to use are rich, fatty meats such as duck. The fat you use to form a seal can be goose, duck or pork fat, clarified butter or oil such as extra virgin or virgin olive, sunflower or canola oil.

Preserves prepared commercially in oil are acidified to prevent micro-organisms from growing and can be stored for several months at room temperature, but when prepared in the home they should be considered a "short-term" preserve and stored in the refrigerator. Herbs, spices and garlic that are packed in bottles of oil for display in the kitchen should be regarded as a pretty decoration and not as a preserve since it is unlikely that they have been prepared for consumption.

After opening, make sure the preserve is always covered in oil. The leftover oil can be strained through a strainer and stored in the refrigerator for a few weeks. It can then be used in salad dressings and marinades, drizzled over warm vegetables, brushed over broiled fish or meat, or used to fry steaks and chicken pieces.

Is it Cooked?

You can cook a batch of plum jam or apple chutney one year and have a completely different experience the next. Every variety of fruit and vegetable differs in how long it takes to cook, and this changes from year to year, too. If you are new to preserve-making, it can take a while to work out when "setting-point" has arrived, or when your preserve is at the right consistency for potting or canning. There are a number of ways to test whether your preserve is cooked.

The natural sugar content, moisture and acidity of a fruit or vegetable are affected by the weather and growing conditions, so one year your tomatoes may need longer to cook, or more sugar adding. Different varieties of a fruit or vegetable vary too; apple varieties, for example, vary hugely in their natural sweetness. Later in the season, fruit and vegetables may be softer and contain more water, or be starchier in texture. This natural variance can affect your set so you do need to be able to work out if your preserve has cooked, rather than rely completely on a recipe time.

The cold saucer method (see page 21) for testing setting points is a useful way for you to gain confidence. You can touch and feel when a preserve is set. I often use three saucers or ramekins when trying a new recipe, which I put in the freezer in advance, so I can test more than once during the cooking time. Once you have made a few preserves, you will feel confident about what a preserve looks like when it has reached setting point.

Jams, marmalades and jellies

Once a jam, marmalade or jelly is at boiling point, continue with a rolling boil until it thickens. A rolling boil has a steady bubbling across the whole surface. At this stage you need to test that "setting point" has been reached and the preserve is cooked. These times vary, so start testing for setting early so that you avoid overcooking the preserve. You should also take the pot off the heat while testing to avoid overcooking. Overcooking will affect the flavor and can prevent setting. If your preserve hasn't yet reached setting point, return it to the burner and boil 5 minutes more, then repeat the test, removing from the burner again.

Chutneys and relishes

To test that a chutney or relish has reached the correct consistency and is cooked, there should be no excess liquid on the surface and the mixture should be thick. If you drag a wooden spoon through the mixture to form a channel, you should be able to see the bottom of the pot. If the channel immediately fills with liquid, it is not cooked. If the channel remains visible for 2 seconds, the preserve is cooked. Retest every few minutes if necessary.

Curds, butters and cheeses

To test that a curd has reached the correct consistency and is cooked, dip a wooden spoon into it; the curd should be creamy and thick enough to coat the back of the spoon. This will happen long before it reaches a boil, which should not be allowed since boiling will curdle and spoil the mixture. A butter is cooked when it is thick enough to spread like jam. Cheeses are cooked when a wooden spoon, drawn across the bottom of the pot, leaves a clear channel through it.

Wrinkle test

Sheet test

Testing for setting point

Your preserve is cooked when it reaches "setting point" and it becomes heavy and glossy. You are then ready to pour it into your sterilized jars.

Wrinkle test

If you don't have a thermometer, put a saucer or ramekin in the freezer before you start cooking. When you think your preserve has reached setting point, take the saucer out of the freezer and put a teaspoon of the preserve on it. Leave it 2 to 3 minutes and, when cool, push it with your finger. If the preserve wrinkles and holds its shape, setting point has been reached. If not, return the pot to the burner for further cooking.

Sheet test

Using a wooden spoon, lift a little of the preserve out of the pan. Twirl the spoon around, let the preserve cool a little and then let the preserve drop back into the pan. If it does not run off the spoon but drops of the preserve run together along the edge of the spoon to form a sheet of drops, setting point has been reached.

Thermometer test

Using a candy thermometer is the most reliable way to test a setting point. When the preserve reaches 221°F, setting point has been reached and you should stop cooking. Preserves that have a high pectin content will reach setting point at a few degrees lower.

Emma's tip When you are ready to test if your preserve is cooked, take the pot off the burner so there is no danger of overcooking. You can always put it back on the burner again if it needs longer to cook.

Canning, Covering & Storing

When your preserve is cooked and you are ready to can it, a few tips on the best way to put it into your sterilized bottles or jars, cover it and store it, will help to keep it at its best.

Canning

In most cases it is best to fill a hot jar with a hot preserve. What you shouldn't do is fill a hot jar with a cold preserve or a cold jar with a hot preserve as the jar might crack. Place the jars on a wooden board as they might crack if on a cold surface when the hot preserve is poured in. Using a funnel if you have one, fill the jar to within ½ inch of the top and, before sealing, tap the jar lightly on a hard surface or run a sterilized spoon through the contents of the jar to release any trapped air pockets that might harbor micro-organisms.

Covering

Cover the jars immediately to prevent bacteria in the air getting in. Screw-top sterilized lids or clip-top lids with a sealing ring provide an effective seal but you can also opt for waxed discs with a cellophane round "lid." Dampen one side of the cellophane round with a clean, damp cloth and put over the hot jar, dampened side uppermost. Pull tightly to seal and secure with an elastic band. When the preserve has cooled, the cover will be tight. It is traditional to cover the cellophane with paper or fabric, tied with string or an elastic band. This works well to

Recommended storage times

Eat your preserves before these times to make sure they taste at their best. After this time, your preserves may start to deteriorate:

Alcoholic preserves	1 month (or 3 years if bottled)
Chutneys, relishes and pickles	1 to 2 years
Curds	2 weeks
Fruit butters	9 months
Fruit cheeses	1 year
Fruit conserves	1 month (or 1 year if bottled)
Fruit liqueurs	2 to 3 years
Jams and jellies	1 year
Marmalades	1 to 2 years
Mincemeats	1 year
Sauces	3 months to 1 year

deter bacteria and looks attractive if you are giving it as a gift. There is no need to use a waxed disc with a lid, unless there is vinegar in your preserve.

Wipe the jars clean with a damp cloth, but, in the case of jams, marmalades and jellies, do not move the preserve until it is set as it may displace pieces of fruit in the preserve or cause uneven cooling, which again can lead to fruit settling or sinking.

Label the preserve with its contents and with the date; you may think that you will remember what is inside the jar but it can be easy to forget. You could add a list of ingredients, too.

Canning

If canning an uncooked preserve, you can pasteurize it using the "waterbath" method so that it lasts longer. Jars covered with cellophane rounds are not suitable for this method. There are two ways to do this: the first is to put the filled jars on a rack in a large pot, making sure that they do not touch each other. Pour in enough water to come halfway up the sides of the jars. Bring the water to a boil, turn the heat down slightly, cover and simmer

1 hour. The second way to pasteurize the filled jars is to steam them in a vegetable steamer 1 hour. Whichever method you use, keep an eye on the water level and top up with more water when needed.

Safe storing

Store preserves in a cool, dry, dark place. Kept in the correct conditions, most preserves can be stored for over a year. Traditionally, most preserves were eaten withina year to make room for next year's preserves. Most pickles, chutneys and relishes should be stored for at least 1 month but preferably for 2 to 3 months before eating to allow their flavor to mature and mellow (cabbage is an exception, see page 17). Once opened, store the preserve in the refrigerator.

Use your own judgement when it comes to deciding if your preserve has deteriorated. If it smells unpleasant, then it probably won't be good to eat! It was once thought that, if mold had developed on the top, the mold could be removed and the remaining preserve was safe to eat. This is now considered a potential health risk and the preserve should be thrown away.

Emma's tip A good-looking label can make all the difference, especially if you are giving the preserve as a gift. You can buy labels ready-made, or if you are feeling creative, buy label paper with a peel-off backing and make your own. Simple designs are often the most effective; a drawing of the fruit or vegetables that are in the preserve can look lovely. If you prefer, a colored line, in the same color as the preserve around the edge of the label to create a frame can look attractive. Choose waterproof markers if hand-writing labels so the information does not deteriorate over time.

Alternatively, tie a cardboard label around the neck of the bottle or jar with string or ribbon. Attractive labels look appealing and professional and reflect the work you have put in.

Troubleshooting

Having spent many hours stirring pots of preserves I felt it would be useful to include a troubleshooting guide so that if something should go wrong during your cooking, you might be able to rescue it. In most cases things only go wrong for me when I have been interrupted or am in a hurry; if you can avoid this, then that will be a great start.

Quick fixes

Preserving is reasonably easy if you follow the basic rules, but every now and again something can go wrong. These are the problems you might encounter while you are making preserves and I give you tips so that you can rectify them, there and then.

Unset jam, jelly or marmlade

If your preserve has not set after cooling, it may be due to undercooking. In this case you can pour it back into the pot and continue to cook until setting point is reached.

Fruit or peel floating to the surface

Fruit or peel floating to the surface

If the fruit or peel rises to the surface of the pot after it has been cooked, let the preserve cool about 15 minutes. This especially applies to jams and marmalades containing large pieces of fruit and thick-cut peel. This gives the fruit time to absorb the sugar, which makes it heavy so that it is suspended in the syrup rather than floating to the surface. Stir well to distribute the fruit or peel and then pour into jars. Conserved fruits in syrup that rise in the jar indicate that they were not packed correctly; they should be tightly packed in a jar of the correct size.

Curds not smooth

The curd has been cooked at too high a temperature and has caused the eggs to curdle. The problem may be rectified by removing it from the heat very quickly and whisking with a balloon whisk until smooth. This may work but will depend upon how badly it's curdled. Curdling can also occur if you do not continue to stir the egg during cooking. This causes bits of egg to coagulate in the mix and they will look white. The only remedy for this is to strain the curd before canning it.

Butters and cheeses too soft

They have not been cooked long enough (see Is it Cooked? page 20). The problem can be solved by further cooking.

Mincemeat fermenting in jar

This can be caused by incorrect storage conditions or inaccurate weighing of ingredients such as too little sugar or lemon juice, too much apple or not enough alcohol. If in doubt, smell and taste the mincemeat. You may be able to rectify fermented mincemeat if you catch it early enough by transferring the mincemeat to a pot, boiling 1 to 2 minutes and adding a splash of brandy or more dried fruit. Pack into newly warmed, sterilized jars, taking care to remove any air bubbles, cover immediately and let cool. Store in the refrigerator or freeze in bags until you need it. Don't just use it for Thanksgiving as it can be added to lots of different desserts and cakes.

Mincemeat drying out

This is probably caused by storing the mincemeat in too warm a place or not having enough liquid to start with; the fruit soaks up more liquid over time. When you want to use the mincemeat, stir in a little alcohol such as sherry or brandy, or the alcohol used in the original recipe, to add moisture.

Liquid collecting at the top of chutney or relish

This is caused because the preserve was not cooked long enough for enough liquid to evaporate. It can be rectified by further cooking. Return it to the pan, bring to a boil and cook until the excess liquid has evaporated. Spoon into warmed, sterilized jars and seal.

Dark-colored pickles

This can occur if you haven't used enough preserving liquid to completely cover the fruit or vegetables. They might look unattractive but there is no cause for alarm and they are safe to eat.

Tips for next time

If a problem has occurred once you have made your preserve, it may just mean that it looks unattractive and doesn't necessarily mean that it has to be thrown away. All is, therefore, not lost, and on a positive note, you will learn from experience and all will be well next time you make it.

Preserve won't set

Lack of pectin is the usual cause if your preserve won't set. This could be due to the type of fruit used, or if the fruit is overripe, in which case the pectin may have deteriorated. Another reason is not cooking the preserve for long enough; it needs time for the pectin to be released and the water to evaporate. Further cooking should rectify this.

Using incorrect proportions of fruit and sugar, and overcooking after adding the sugar are other reasons the preserve has failed to set, but this cannot be rectified.

If the jam hasn't set after canning, return it to the pot, add the juice of 1 small lemon and return to a boil. Test for a set and, when setting point has been reached, ladle into warmed, sterilized jars and seal.

Mold on the surface

This can be caused by not sterilizing the jars correctly; for example, if the jars are damp or cold. Not canning the preserve while it is still hot and not covering it immediately can also cause the development of mold, along with not filling jars to the top. Storing a preserve in a very warm or damp place can lead to mold, too. When making pickles, always wash the fruit or vegetables well because they are not cooked and any micro-organisms remaining may lead to mold. It is not advised to eat a preserve that has mold on it.

Preserve has crystallized

Not allowing the sugar to dissolve completely before bringing the preserve to a boil, or using too much sugar, can cause crystallization. It cannot be remedied but the preserve is still safe to eat. Since it will taste sweet and have a crunchy texture it is ideally best used in cooking. If crystals have formed on top of the preserve after it has been opened, they are caused by evaporation of liquid.

Shrinking from sides of jar

This is due to evaporation and is caused by not making the preserve airtight when covering. Over-boiling during cooking can also cause the preserve to shrink from the sides of the jar, as can storing the jar in a too warm, damp, or light place. The best solution is to eat the preserve as soon as possible.

Chutney, relish, jam, marmalade or jelly has a burnt flavor

This occurs when the preserve is not stirred enough during cooking and some has stuck to the bottom of the pot, causing it to burn. There is no remedy for this, and having done this plenty of times in the past, my only advice is to give yourself lots of time to cook and never walk away from a boiling pot!

Dull color in preserves

Dullness is caused either by cooking the jam for too long before adding the sugar, or boiling it for too long once it has been added. It's fine to eat but just not sparkling and attractive.

Fading color in preserves

Fading especially applies to red fruits such as strawberries and raspberries. Incorrect storage is the problem and has been caused by storing the preserve in a too light or warm place, or storing it for too long. It may still be all right to eat, so taste a little to be sure.

Darkening at the top of jar

This can occur if the preserve is not sealed and indicates that air has gotten in, causing oxidation. This can occur naturally over time with light-colored preserves and chutneys and is perfectly safe. Give it a quick stir before serving to improve the appearance. This problem can also occur if the preserve has been incorrectly stored in too warm or light a place. If there are other signs of deterioration then do not eat, but if you are sure it is just due to storage, then it is safe to eat.

Bubbles in jam, jellies and marmalades

This can be an indication that fermentation has occurred during storage; the jam may also smell gassy when

Bubbles in jam, jellies and marmalades

you remove the lid. It can be due to the jars not being sterilized or sealed correctly. It can also be caused by too little sugar in the finished product, undercooking of the jam, or inaccurate measuring of the ingredients. This problem may have been apparent earlier since the preserve would not have set correctly. If the jam has fermented, it should not be eaten.

If there is no indication of fermentation, bubbles may just be caught in the scum that often forms during cooking. This preserve is safe to eat but just does not look as good as it could. Swirling 1 teaspoon of butter into the jam at the end of cooking can help to reduce and disperse scum. You can also just skim off the scum with a metal spoon before canning.

Weeping jams, jellies and marmalades
Caused because the preserve was stored in too warm a place or the storage temperature fluctuated. The preserve can still be eaten but will be soft.

Tough peel in marmalade
The peel wasn't cooked for long enough before adding the sugar, which then further hardens the peel. Unfortunately, the problem can't be rectified.

Jelly too stiff
The jelly contained too much pectin because the fruit was under-ripe or it was overcooked. Next time, use ripe fruit and test for a set earlier.

Jelly looks cloudy
Chances are you poked or squeezed the bag while the liquid was dripping and this has caused it to go cloudy. It cannot be rectified but the jelly will still be edible. Let the jelly drip at its own pace next time. Jelly can also look cloudy if you used under-ripe fruit, which can release its starch and turn the jelly cloudy.

Chutney, relish or pickle has a metallic flavor
The preserve has been cooked in a brass or copper preserving pan, which imparts a metallic flavor due to the reaction of the pan with the vinegar. In future, use an aluminum or stainless steel pan.

Soft or tough pickles
Soft pickles can be caused by using vinegar with low acidity or not enough salt, whereas too much salting can cause tough pickles. This can also occur if you decide to pasteurize your pickles in a hot water bath or you keep them for a long time before eating (over 12 months). Always use a vinegar with a 5 to 7 percent acid content and measure the salt accurately. Storing in a warm place will also cause pickles to soften.

Jams & Marmalades

Raspberry Jam

Serve this classic jam spread on toast or scones for a delicious taste of summer, or in Bakewell and jam tarts. You could also serve a spoonful with vanilla ice cream or hot vanilla pudding for a quick dessert. This recipe also works well with loganberries.

2 pounds, 4 ounces (8 cups) raspberries
juice of 1 lemon

5 cups granulated sugar
1 teaspoon butter

MAKES ABOUT: 4 pounds (6 to 6½ cups) PREPARATION TIME: 20 minutes COOKING TIME: 20 minutes

1 Put the raspberries and lemon juice in a preserving pan and slowly raise the heat until the juices start to run. Simmer gently 5 minutes to allow the raspberries to soften slightly.

2 If you prefer a seedless jam, push the raspberries through a fine mesh strainer and return to the pan. Discard the seeds left in the strainer.

3 Add the sugar to the pan and stir until completely dissolved. Bring to a boil and boil rapidly about 10 minutes until setting point is reached. Test for a set either with a candy thermometer (it should read 221°F) or put a teaspoon of the jam onto a cold saucer and let it cool a few minutes. If it wrinkles when you push it with your finger, then it is ready to use.

4 Meanwhile, sterilize enough jars in the oven so that they are ready to use (see page 14).

5 Remove the pan from the heat. Swirl in the butter. If any scum remains, skim with a slotted spoon.

6 Ladle the jam into the warmed, sterilized jars. Cover immediately with sterilized lids. Label and store in a cool, dry, dark place. Refrigerate after opening.

Morello Cherry (Sour Cherry) Jam

Dark red morello cherries (or any sour cherries) are excellent for cooking as they have a concentrated cherry flavor. This recipe also works well with sweet dessert cherries.

3 lemons

2 pounds, 4 ounces (5 cups) morello cherries or any sour cherries, pitted

5 cups granulated sugar

1 teaspoon butter

MAKES ABOUT: 3 pounds, 12 ounces (5½ to 6 cups) PREPARATION TIME: 20 minutes
COOKING TIME: 45 minutes

1 Using a sharp knife or potato peeler, pare the zest from the lemons and then slice the zest very finely. Cut the lemons in half and squeeze out the juice and seeds. Tie the seeds in a piece of cheesecloth.

2 Put the lemon zest, lemon juice, cheesecloth bag and 5 cups water in a preserving pan and slowly bring to a boil.

3 Reduce the heat and simmer about 10 minutes until the liquid is reduced by two thirds and the zest is soft.

4 Remove the cheesecloth bag from the pan, squeezing it well and allowing the juices to run back into the pan. Discard the bag.

5 Add the cherries and simmer about 20 minutes until soft.

6 Add the sugar to the pan and stir until completely dissolved. Bring to a boil and boil rapidly 10 to 15 minutes until setting point is reached. Test for a set either with a candy thermometer (it should read 221°F) or put a teaspoon of the jam onto a cold saucer and let it cool a few minutes. If it wrinkles when you push it with your finger, then it is ready to use.

7 Meanwhile, sterilize enough jars in the oven so that they are ready to use (see page 14).

8 Remove the pan from the heat. Swirl in the butter. If any scum remains, skim with a slotted spoon.

9 Ladle the jam into the warmed, sterilized jars and cover immediately with sterilized lids. Label and store in a cool, dry, dark place. Refrigerate after opening.

Emma's tip It would be worth investing in a cherry pitter for this recipe as it really does save time. Alternatively, you can cook the cherries with their pits in and remove them from the pan with a slotted spoon as they float to the surface, before adding the sugar.

The Best Strawberry Jam

The flavor of summer, packed into a jar. Strawberries lack pectin, which means this jam needs jelly sugar to set. Serve it spread on scones with clotted cream for a "cream tea," use it to sandwich a layer cake, or indulge in a spoonful right from the jar.

2 pounds, 4 ounces (about 8 to 9 cups) small
  strawberries, or large strawberries, cut in half
juice of 2 lemons
2¾ cups granulated sugar

2 cups jelly sugar with added pectin
1 teaspoon butter

MAKES ABOUT: 3 pounds, 12 ounces (5½ to 6 cups) PREPARATION TIME: 25 minutes, plus 15 minutes cooling COOKING TIME: 15 minutes

1 Put the strawberries and lemon juice in a preserving pan and slowly raise the heat until the juices start to run. Simmer gently 5 minutes for the strawberries to soften slightly.

2 Add the granulated sugar and jelly sugar to the pan and stir until completely dissolved. Bring to a boil and boil rapidly 6 to 8 minutes until setting point is reached. Test for a set either with a candy thermometer (it should read 221°F) or put a teaspoon of the jam onto a cold saucer and let it cool a few minutes. If it wrinkles when you push it with your finger, then it is ready to use.

3 Meanwhile, sterilize enough jars in the oven so that they are ready to use (see page 14).

4 Remove the pan from the heat. Swirl in the butter. If any scum remains, skim with a slotted spoon. Let the jam cool 15 minutes (this will help to prevent the fruit from rising in the jars).

5 Ladle the jam into the warmed, sterilized jars. Cover immediately with sterilized lids. Label and store in a cool, dry, dark place. Refrigerate after opening.

Emma's tip Using whole small strawberries makes a beautiful jam, which is perfect for spooning onto scones, but you can use large strawberries sliced in half, too. You might like to invest in a strawberry huller as it really does make the strawberry preparation simpler.

Black Currant Jam

This jam, with its intense, fruity flavor, is delicious served spread on bread or toast. You could also try a spoonful with crêpes, drop scones, rice pudding or yogurt.

2 pounds, 4 ounces (about 10 cups) black currants, stripped from their vines

7½ cups granulated sugar
1 teaspoon butter

MAKES ABOUT: 5 pounds, 8 ounces (8½ to 9 cups) PREPARATION TIME: 15 minutes, plus 15 minutes cooling COOKING TIME: 1 hour

1 Put the black currants and 3¾ cups water in a preserving pan and slowly bring to a boil.

2 Reduce the heat and simmer gently about 45 minutes until the black currants are very soft but have not disintegrated into a pulp, and the liquid is well reduced. Stir from time to time to prevent the mixture from sticking to the bottom of the pan.

3 Add the sugar to the pan and stir until completely dissolved. Bring to a boil and boil rapidly about 10 minutes, or until setting point is reached. Test for a set either with a candy thermometer (it should read 221°F) or put a teaspoon of the jam onto a cold saucer and let cool a few minutes. If it wrinkles when you push it with your finger, then it is ready to use.

4 Meanwhile, sterilize enough jars in the oven so that they are ready to use (see page 14).

5 Take the pan off the heat. Swirl in the butter. If any scum remains, skim with a slotted spoon. Allow the jam to cool 15 minutes (this will help to prevent the fruit from rising in the jars).

6 Ladle the jam into the warmed, sterilized jars and cover immediately with sterilized lids. Label and store in a cool, dry, dark place. Refrigerate after opening.

Strawberry & Rhubarb Jam

Strawberries and rhubarb are in season at the same time and make a happy marriage. The strawberries sweeten the tart rhubarb and it makes a good jam to serve as a breakfast spread or spooned on top of yogurt.

2 pounds, 4 ounces (about 8 to 9 cups) small strawberries, or large strawberries, cut in half
2 pounds, 4 ounces (about 10 cups) rhubarb, sliced into ½-inch pieces

7½ cups granulated sugar
juice of 2 lemons
juice of 1 orange
1 teaspoon butter

MAKES ABOUT: 4 pounds, 8 ounces (7 cups) PREPARATION TIME: 20 minutes, plus 15 minutes cooling
COOKING TIME: 40 minutes

1 Put the strawberries and rhubarb in a preserving pan and heat gently until the juices start to run.

2 Slowly bring to a boil, then reduce the heat and simmer gently about 20 minutes until the fruits are soft and the liquid is well reduced. Stir from time to time to prevent the mixture from sticking to the bottom of the pan.

3 Add the sugar to the pan and stir until completely dissolved. Add the lemon and orange juice, bring to a boil and boil rapidly about 15 minutes, or until setting point is reached. Test for a set either with a candy thermometer (it should read 221°F) or put a teaspoon of the jam onto a cold saucer and let cool

a few minutes. If it wrinkles when you push it with your finger, then it is ready to use.

4 Meanwhile, sterilize enough jars in the oven so that they are ready to use (see page 14).

5 Take the pan off the heat. Swirl in the butter. If any scum remains, skim with a slotted spoon. Let the jam cool 15 minutes (this will help to prevent the fruit from rising in the jars).

6 Ladle the jam into the warmed, sterilized jars and cover immediately with sterilized lids. Label and store in a cool, dry, dark place. Refrigerate after opening.

Emma's tip Vanilla complements both strawberries and rhubarb and you need just a hint to flavor the jam. Split a vanilla bean in half, scrape out the seeds, and add both the seeds and bean to the fruit at the beginning of cooking. Remove the bean before cooling.

High Dumpsideary Jam

It is thought that this jam gets its unusual name from a Mrs. Dumpsideary. Finding there was nothing left to put on her toast, Mr. Dumpsideary solves the problem by making his wife a jam from windfall autumn fruit and spices that he had in the cupboard. It is a very useful recipe if you have a glut of plums, apples and pears.

1 pound, 2 ounces (about 2½ to 3 cups) plums, roughly chopped, and pits reserved
grated zest and juice of 1 lemon
marble-sized piece ginger root, bruised
2 cloves
1 cinnamon stick
1 pound, 2 ounces (about 5 cups) cooking apples, peeled, cored and roughly chopped

1 pound, 2 ounces (about 5 cups) firm, under-ripe pears, peeled, cored and roughly chopped
3 tablespoons raisins
6½ cups granulated sugar
1 teaspoon butter

MAKES ABOUT: 8 pounds, 4 ounces (13 cups)   PREPARATION TIME: 45 minutes
COOKING TIME: 45 minutes

1 Tie the plum pits, lemon zest, ginger, cloves and cinnamon in a piece of cheesecloth.

2 Put the cheesecloth bag and all the ingredients, except the sugar and butter, in a preserving pan. Add ⅔ cup water and slowly bring to a boil. Reduce the heat and simmer gently 20 to 30 minutes, depending on the ripeness of the fruit, until they are soft. Stir from time to time to prevent the mixture from sticking to the bottom of the pan.

3 Remove the cheesecloth bag from the pan, squeezing it well and letting the juice run back into the pan. Discard the bag.

4 Add the sugar to the pan and stir until completely dissolved. Bring to a boil and boil rapidly about

15 minutes or until setting point is reached. Test for a set either with a candy thermometer (it should read 221°F) or put a teaspoon of the jam onto a cold saucer and let it cool a few minutes. If it wrinkles when you push it with your finger, then it is ready to use.

5 Meanwhile, sterilize enough jars in the oven so that they are ready to use (see page 14).

6 Remove the pan from the heat. Swirl in the butter. If any scum remains, skim with a slotted spoon.

7 Ladle the jam into the warmed, sterilized jars. Cover immediately with sterilized lids. Label and store in a cool, dry, dark place. Refrigerate after opening.

Spiced Victoria Plum Jam

You can use whichever variety of plums you have to make this jam. At the Bay Tree Food Company in Somerset, England, we use Victoria plums but any small, sweet plums will be delicious, too, although of course the color may differ. Just make sure your plums are very ripe.

2 pounds, 4 ounces Victoria plums or other small plums, cut in half, and pits reserved
2 cinnamon sticks, broken in half
4 whole cloves

juice of 1 lemon
5 cups granulated sugar
1 teaspoon butter

MAKES ABOUT: 3 pounds, 12 ounces (5½ to 6 cups) PREPARATION TIME: 40 minutes, plus 15 minutes cooling COOKING TIME: 45 minutes

1 Tie the plum pits, cinnamon sticks and cloves in a piece of cheesecloth.

2 Put the plums, cheesecloth bag and lemon juice in a preserving pan. Add 1¼ cups water and slowly bring to a boil. Reduce the heat and simmer gently 20 to 30 minutes, depending on the ripeness of the plums, until the fruit and skins are soft. Stir from time to time to prevent the mixture from sticking to the bottom of the pan.

3 Remove the cheesecloth bag from the pan, squeezing it well and allowing the juice to run back into the pan. Discard the bag.

4 Add the sugar to the pan and stir until completely dissolved. Bring to a boil and boil rapidly 10 to 15 minutes until setting point is reached. If the plums are rising to the surface, cook for another

2 to 4 minutes for the plums to absorb more of the sugar. Test for a set either with a candy thermometer (it should read 221°F) or put a teaspoon of the jam onto a cold saucer and let cool a few minutes. If it wrinkles when you push it with your finger, then it is ready to use.

5 Meanwhile, sterilize enough jars in the oven so that they are ready to use (see page 14).

6 Remove the pan from the heat. Swirl in the butter. If any scum remains, skim with a slotted spoon. Let the jam cool 15 minutes (this will help to prevent the fruit from rising in the jars).

7 Ladle the jam into the warmed, sterilized jars and cover immediately with sterilized lids. Label and store in a cool, dry, dark place. Refrigerate after opening.

Wild Apricot & Almond Jam

Using hard, dried Hunza apricots that come from wild apricot trees in the Hunza valley, Pakistan, creates a jam with an intense, toffee-like flavor. You need to soak the apricots beforehand overnight, but otherwise this is a very simple recipe. This is the jam to serve with warmed croissants in the morning.

1 pound (about 2½ cups) dried Hunza apricots
juice of 1 lemon
6½ cups granulated sugar

scant ½ cup blanched almonds, halved
1 teaspoon butter

MAKES ABOUT: 5 pounds (8 cups)   PREPARATION TIME: 20 minutes, plus 12 hours soaking
COOKING TIME: 1 hour

1 Put the apricots in a large bowl. Add 7½ cups water and let soak 12 hours.

2 The next day, put the soaked apricots and the water in a preserving pan. Add the lemon juice and slowly bring to a boil. Reduce the heat and simmer gently about 30 minutes until the apricots are soft. Stir from time to time to prevent the mixture from sticking to the bottom of the pan.

3 Add the sugar and almonds to the pan and stir until the sugar has completely dissolved. Bring to a boil and boil rapidly 20 to 25 minutes until setting point is reached. Test for a set either with a candy thermometer (it should read 221°F) or put a teaspoon of the jam onto a cold saucer and let cool a few minutes. If it wrinkles when you push it with your finger, then it is ready to use.

4 Meanwhile, sterilize enough jars in the oven so that they are ready to use (see page 14).

5 Remove the pan from the heat. Swirl in the butter. If any scum remains, skim with a slotted spoon.

6 Ladle the jam into the warmed, sterilized jars and cover immediately with sterilized lids. Label and store in a cool, dry, dark place. Refrigerate after opening.

Emma's tip If you can't find Hunza apricots then substitute with organic dried apricots. Pre-soaked, plump "ready-to-eat" apricots won't have the same rich flavor.

Billy Banana Jam

The Fruit Orchard Kids were jam jars, cookie jars and statues that were made in the United States in 1942. There were six in total, the others being Stella Strawberry, Charlie Cherry, Lee Lemon, Albert Apple and Penny Pineapple. We've used the name for this delicious jam. Spread it on fresh bread or combine it with peanut butter in a sandwich.

2 pounds, 4 pounds ripe bananas (6 to 7 medium), peeled

scant 3½ cups granulated sugar
juice of 1 lemon

MAKES ABOUT: 2 pounds, 4 ounces (3½ cups) PREPARATION TIME: 15 minutes
COOKING TIME: 20 minutes

1 Put the bananas in a food processor and blend to make a rough puree.

2 Put the banana puree in a preserving pan and add the sugar and lemon juice. Slowly bring to a boil, stirring all the time to prevent the mixture from sticking to the bottom of the pan. Reduce the heat and continue stirring 10 to 15 minutes until the mixture is thick. The jam is ready when a wooden spoon drawn across the bottom of the pan reveals the bottom cleanly. (There is no need to test for a set.)

3 Meanwhile, sterilize enough jars in the oven so that they are ready to use (see page 14).

4 Ladle the jam into the warmed, sterilized jars. Cover immediately with sterilized lids. Label and store in a cool, dry, dark place. Refrigerate after opening.

Emma's tip This is a good way to use up very ripe bananas (under-ripe bananas will be too starchy for this recipe). You can spread it on bread but it is also delicious used as a topping on ice cream, crêpes and waffles. You could try spicing it up by adding ½ teaspoon ground cloves, 1 teaspoon ground cinnamon, 1 teaspoon cardamom or 1 teaspoon vanilla extract. You can also add ½ cup chopped walnuts or ½ cup dried currants at the end of cooking. For a caramel flavor you could use light brown sugar instead of granulated sugar.

Spiced Carrot Jam

Vegetable jams are popular in the Middle East and lend themselves to the addition of spices. This is a delicious way to preserve an abundant crop of carrots. Serve it on crusty bread or on a bagel with cream cheese.

2 pounds, 4 ounces (7 to 7½ cups) carrots, grated
grated zest and juice of 1 lemon
grated zest and juice of 2 oranges
1 teaspoon ground cinnamon

½ teaspoon ground cloves
¼ teaspoon grated nutmeg
5 cups granulated sugar
1 teaspoon butter

MAKES ABOUT: 3 pounds, 12 ounces (5½ to 6 cups)   PREPARATION TIME: 30 minutes
COOKING TIME: 55 minutes

1 Put the carrots, lemon and orange zests and juices, cinnamon, cloves and nutmeg in a preserving pan. Add 3¾ cups water and slowly bring to a boil. Reduce the heat and simmer about 20 minutes until the carrots are tender and the liquid is well reduced. Stir from time to time to prevent the mixture from sticking to the bottom of the pan.

2 Add the sugar to the pan and stir until the sugar has completely dissolved. Bring to a boil and boil rapidly about 30 minutes or until setting point is reached. Test for a set either with a candy thermometer (it should read 221°F) or put a teaspoon of the jam onto a cold saucer and let cool a few minutes. If it wrinkles when you push it with your finger, then it is ready to use.

3 Meanwhile, sterilize enough jars in the oven so that they are ready to use (see page 14).

4 Remove the pan from the heat and pack the carrot well into the warmed, sterilized jars, topping up with the liquid. Cover immediately with sterilized lids. Label and store in a cool, dry, dark place. Refrigerate after opening.

Butternut Squash, Ginger & Citrus Jam

This vibrant, orange jam tastes rich and zesty and has a soft, spreading consistency. It isn't too sweet and tastes good spread on toast as well as muffins and pancakes. It can even be used in a chicken or turkey sandwich in the same way as you would use chutney.

3 pounds, 5 ounces butternut squash, peeled and
  seeded
3½ ounces (about ¾ cup) ginger root, peeled and
  finely sliced into small pieces
grated zest and juice of 3 lemons

grated zest and juice of 4 oranges
grated zest and juice of 1 lime
1 teaspoon ground ginger
½ teaspoon ground cinnamon
4 cups granulated sugar

MAKES ABOUT: 4 pounds (6 cups) PREPARATION TIME: 35 minutes COOKING TIME: 55 minutes

1 Grate the butternut squash, either by hand or in a food processor.

2 Put all the ingredients, except the sugar, in a preserving pan. Add 4¼ cups water and slowly bring to a boil.

3 Reduce the heat and simmer about 20 minutes until the squash is soft. Stir from time to time to prevent the mixture from sticking to the bottom of the pan.

4 Add the sugar to the pan and stir until completely dissolved. Bring to a boil and boil rapidly about

30 minutes until no excess liquid remains and the mixture is thick. Stir from time to time. The jam is ready when a wooden spoon drawn across the bottom of the pan reveals the bottom cleanly. (There is no need to test for a set.)

5 Meanwhile, sterilize enough jars in the oven so that they are ready to use (see page 14).

6 Ladle the jam into the warmed, sterilized jars. Cover immediately with sterilized lids. Label and store in a cool, dry, dark place. Refrigerate after opening.

Emma's tip Pumpkins also work well in this recipe and, if you are making jack-o'-lanterns for Halloween, it is a great way of using up the flesh. The jam would be lovely spread on cupcakes or cookies, and you could add a ghost or spider decoration, too!

Sweet Tomato Chili Jam

This fiery, flecked red jam is really a relish and it goes with a range of dishes. Try it with cold meats, bread and cheese or barbecued burgers. You can also serve it alongside fishcakes to add a little gentle heat.

2 pounds, 4 ounces tomatoes (about 6 to
   7 medium)
juice of 2 lemons

2 teaspoons dried red pepper flakes
¼ teaspoon sea salt
5 cups granulated sugar

MAKES ABOUT: 3 pounds, 2 ounces (4½ to 5 cups)   PREPARATION TIME: 35 minutes, plus 15 minutes cooling
COOKING TIME: 25 minutes

1 With a sharp knife, cut a cross in the top of each tomato. Put the tomatoes in a heatproof bowland cover with boiling water. Let stand 2 to 3 minutes, then drain. Peel off and discard the skins. Roughly chop the flesh.

2 Put the tomatoes, lemon juice, red pepper flakes and sea salt in a preserving pan and bring to a boil. Reduce the heat and simmer 5 minutes until the tomatoes are softened.

3 Add the sugar to the pan and stir until the sugar has completely dissolved. Bring to a boil and boil rapidly 10 to 15 minutes until setting point is reached. Test for a set either with a candy thermometer (it should read 221°F) or put a teaspoon of the jam onto a cold saucer and let cool a few minutes. If it wrinkles when you push it with your finger, then it is ready to use.

4 Meanwhile, sterilize enough jars in the oven so that they are ready to use (see page 14).

5 Remove the pan from the heat and let the jam cool 15 minutes (this helps to prevent the tomatoes from rising in the jars).

6 Ladle the jam into the warmed, sterilized jars and cover immediately with sterilized lids. Label and store in a cool, dry, dark place. Refrigerate after opening.

Rose Petal Jam

Known as Gulkand in India, where it is very popular, Rose Petal Jam is made by leaving the petals in full sunshine. This is a version that doesn't rely on such demands. It is, however, a jam to make if you have an abundance of red roses. Serve at a summer afternoon tea on cookies or meringues, or use as a cake filling with the addition of whipped cream and fresh strawberries or raspberries. You could scatter the tablecloth with extra rose petals!

8 ounces freshly picked, dark red, heavily-scented
  rose blooms
2½ cups granulated sugar

juice of 2 lemons
a few drops of culinary rose extract (optional)

MAKES ABOUT: 1 pound, 5 ounces (2 cups)   PREPARATION TIME: 30 minutes, plus 12 hours standing
COOKING TIME: 50 minutes

1 Remove the petals from the rose blooms and snip off and discard the white bases. Cut the petals into small pieces and put in a bowl.

2 Add 1¼ cups of the sugar to the petals. Cover and let stand at room temperature 12 hours or overnight to extract the rose flavor and darken the petals.

3 The next day, put the lemon juice, 5 cups water and the remaining sugar in a heavy pot. Gently heat the mixture, stirring until the sugar has dissolved, but do not boil.

4 Stir in the rose petal mixture and simmer gently 30 minutes. Slowly bring to a boil and boil rapidly

about 15 minutes until thick. (There is no need to test for a set.)

5 Meanwhile, sterilize enough jars in the oven so that they are ready to use (see page 14).

6 Remove the pan from the heat and remove any scum with a slotted spoon. Taste (be careful as it will be hot), and if the jam doesn't have a distinct rose flavor, add a few drops of rose extract.

7 Ladle the jam into the warmed, sterilized jars. Cover immediately with sterilized lids. Label and store in a cool, dry, dark place. Refrigerate after opening.

Emma's tip You will need about 16 rose blooms to make up the weight required for this recipe.

Traditional Seville Orange Marmalade

The season for Seville oranges (bitter oranges) is short, so make a batch of this marmalade in late winter or freeze the fruit and make it when convenient. Serve on hot buttered toast for a really refreshing start to the day, and it will remind you how marmalade should taste.

3 pounds, 5 ounces Seville oranges (bitter oranges)
juice of 2 lemons

15 cups granulated sugar

MAKES ABOUT: 11 pounds (17 cups) PREPARATION TIME: 45 minutes, plus 20 minutes cooling
COOKING TIME: 2 hours, 20 minutes

1 Cut the oranges in half and squeeze out the juice and seeds. Tie the seeds, and any extra membrane that has come away during squeezing, in some cheesecloth.

2 Either by hand or using the shredding attachment of a food processor, slice the orange peel, with its pith, into thin, medium or thick shreds, according to your preference.

3 Put the orange juice and peel, lemon juice, cheesecloth bag and 15 cups water in a preserving pan and slowly bring to a boil. Reduce the heat and simmer gently about 2 hours until the peel is very soft and the liquid reduced by about half.

4 Remove the cheesecloth bag from the pan and let cool 5 minutes before squeezing it well and allowing the juices to run back into the pan. Discard the bag.

5 Add the sugar to the pan and stir until completely dissolved. Bring to a boil and boil rapidly about 15 minutes, or until setting point is reached. Test for a set either with a candy thermometer (it should read 221°F) or put a teaspoon of the marmalade onto a cold saucer and let cool a few minutes. If it wrinkles when you push it with your finger, then it is ready to use.

6 Meanwhile, sterilize enough jars in the oven so that they are ready to use (see page 14).

7 Remove the pan from the heat and skim with a slotted spoon to remove any scum. Let cool 15 minutes (this will help to prevent the peel from rising in the jars).

8 Ladle the marmalade into the warmed, sterilized jars and cover immediately with sterilized lids. Label and store in a cool, dry, dark place. Refrigerate after opening.

Emma's tip Tart Seville oranges (bitter oranges) are best for marmalade as they produce a good flavor and contain more pectin than sweet oranges. Marmalades made with sweet oranges will have a cloudier appearance.

Lime & Lemon Shred Marmalade

The combination of these two citrus fruits produces a refreshing, zesty marmalade.
Use it to spread on toast or to flavor homemade breakfast muffins.

1 pound, 2 ounces limes
9 ounces lemons

7½ cups granulated sugar

MAKES ABOUT: 5 pounds (8 cups)   PREPARATION TIME: 45 minutes, plus 20 minutes cooling
COOKING TIME: 1 hour 45 minutes

1 Cut the limes and lemons in half and squeeze out the juice and seeds. Tie the seeds, and any extra membrane that has come away during squeezing, in some cheesecloth.

2 Either by hand or using the shredding attachment of a food processor, thinly slice the lime and lemon peel, with its pith, into shreds.

3 Put the lime and lemon juice and peel, cheesecloth bag and 7½ cups water in a preserving pan and slowly bring to a boil. Reduce the heat and simmer gently about 1½ hours until the peel is very soft and the liquid reduced by half.

4 Remove the cheesecloth bag from the pan and let cool 5 minutes before squeezing it well and allowing the juices to run back into the pan. Discard the bag.

5 Add the sugar to the pan and stir until the sugar is completely dissolved. Bring to a boil and boil rapidly about 10 minutes or until setting point is reached.

Test for a set either with a candy thermometer (it should read 221°F) or put a teaspoon of the marmalade onto a cold saucer and let cool a few minutes. If it wrinkles when you push it with your finger, then it is ready to use.

6 Meanwhile, sterilize enough jars in the oven so that they are ready to use (see page 14).

7 Remove the pan from the heat and skim with a slotted spoon to remove any scum. Let cool 15 minutes (this will help to prevent the peel from rising in the jars).

8 Ladle the marmalade into the warmed, sterilized jars and cover immediately with sterilized lids. Label and store in a cool, dry, dark place. Refrigerate after opening.

Orange, Lemon & Ginger Marmalade

Ginger adds a warming kick to marmalade. Delicious on toast, this marmalade is also good stirred into plain yogurt or used in baked desserts.

1 pound, 2 ounces oranges

13 ounces lemons

4 ounces (¾ to 1 cup) ginger root, peeled and finely sliced into small pieces

1 tablespoon ginger paste

5 cups granulated sugar

MAKES ABOUT: 4 pounds, 3 ounces (6½ to 7 cups) PREPARATION TIME: 45 minutes, plus 15 minutes cooling
COOKING TIME: 1¾ to 2¼ hours

1 Cut the oranges and lemons in half and squeeze out the juice and seeds. Tie the seeds, and any extra membrane that has come away during squeezing, in a double thickness of cheesecloth.

2 Either by hand or using the shredding attachment of a food processor, thinly slice the orange and lemon peel, with its pith, into thin, medium or thick shreds, according to your preference.

3 Put the orange and lemon juice and peel, cheesecloth bag and 10 cups water in a preserving pan and slowly bring to a boil. Reduce the heat and simmer gently 1½ to 2 hours until the peel is soft and the liquid reduced by about half.

4 Remove the cheesecloth bag from the pan and let cool 5 minutes before squeezing it well and allowing the juice to run back into the pan. Discard the bag.

5 Add the ginger, ginger paste and sugar to the pan and stir until the sugar has completely dissolved. Bring to a boil and boil rapidly about 15 minutes, or until setting point is reached. Test for a set either with a candy thermometer (it should read 221°F) or put a teaspoon of the marmalade onto a cold saucer and let cool a few minutes. If it wrinkles when you push it with your finger, then it is ready to use.

6 Meanwhile, sterilize enough jars in the oven so that they are ready to use (see page 14).

7 Remove the pan from the heat and skim with a slotted spoon to remove any scum. Let cool 15 minutes (this will help to prevent the shreds from rising in the jars).

8 Ladle the marmalade into the warmed, sterilized jars and cover immediately with sterilized lids. Label and store in a cool, dry, dark place. Refrigerate after opening.

Lemon & Lavender Marmalade

Lavender's strong flavor complements that of sharp citrus fruits, making it the perfect pairing with lemons. Serve this marmalade with toast or muffins.

1 pound, 10 ounces lemons
2 teaspoon dried or ¾ teaspoon fresh culinary lavender flowers

7½ cups granulated sugar
½ teaspoon lavender essence

MAKES ABOUT: 5 pounds (8 cups)   PREPARATION TIME: 45 minutes, plus 15 minutes cooling
COOKING TIME: 1¾ to 2¼ hours

1 Cut the lemons in half and squeeze out the juice and seeds. Tie the seeds, and any extra membrane that has come away during squeezing, in a double thickness of cheesecloth.

2 Either by hand or using the shredding attachment of a food processor, thinly slice the lemon peel, with its pith, into shreds.

3 Put the lemon juice and peel, cheesecloth bag and 7½ cups water in a preserving pan and slowly bring to a boil. Reduce the heat and simmer gently 1½ to 2 hours until the peel is really soft and the liquid reduced by about half.

4 Remove the cheesecloth bag from the pan and let cool 5 minutes before squeezing it well and allowing the juices to run back into the pan. Discard the bag.

5 Add the lavender flowers and sugar to the pan and stir until the sugar has completely dissolved. Bring

to a boil and boil rapidly about 15 minutes or until setting point is reached. Test for a set either with a candy thermometer (it should read 221°F) or put a teaspoon of the marmalade onto a cold saucer and let cool a few minutes. If it wrinkles when you push it with your finger, then it is ready to use.

6 Meanwhile, sterilize enough jars in the oven so that they are ready to use (see page 14).

7 Remove the pan from the heat and skim with a slotted spoon to remove any scum. Stir in the lavender essence. Let cool 15 minutes (this will help to prevent the peel from rising in the jars).

8 Ladle the marmalade into the warmed, sterilized jars and cover immediately with sterilized lids. Label and store in a cool, dry, dark place. Refrigerate after opening.

Emma's tip You can buy culinary lavender flowers from specialty lavender farms and online merchants. If you grow lavender yourself, you need to be sure the plants have never been sprayed with insecticide before you decide to cook with them.

Pink Grapefruit & Elderflower Marmalade

Grapefruit and elderflower complement each other very well, and make a refreshing marmalade. Pink grapefruit tends to be sweeter than yellow grapefruit but you can use either in this recipe.

2 pounds, 4 ounces pink grapefruits
1 pound, 2 ounces lemons

6½ cups granulated sugar
6 tablespoons elderflower syrup

MAKES ABOUT: 6 pounds (9 to 9½ cups) PREPARATION TIME: 45 minutes plus 15 minutes cooling
COOKING TIME: 1¾ to 2¼ hours

1 Cut the grapefruits and lemons and squeeze out the juice and seeds. Tie the seeds, and any extra membrane that has come away during squeezing, in a double thickness of cheesecloth.

2 Either by hand or using the shredding attachment of a food processor, thinly slice the grapefruit and lemon peel, with its pith, into shreds.

3 Put the grapefruit and lemon juice and peel, cheesecloth bag and 7½ cups water in a preserving pan and slowly bring to a boil. Reduce the heat and simmer gently 1½ to 2 hours until the peel is soft and the liquid reduced by about half.

4 Remove the cheesecloth bag from the pan and let cool 5 minutes before squeezing it well and allowing the juices to run back into the pan. Discard the bag.

5 Add the sugar to the pan and stir until the sugar is completely dissolved. Bring to a boil and boil rapidly about 15 minutes, or until setting point is reached. Test for a set either with a candy thermometer (it should read 221°F) or put a teaspoon of the marmalade onto a cold saucer and let cool a few minutes. If it wrinkles when you push it with your finger, then it is ready to use.

6 Meanwhile, sterilize enough jars in the oven so that they are ready to use (see page 14).

7 Remove the pan from the heat and skim with a slotted spoon to remove any scum. Stir in the elderflower cordial. Let cool 15 minutes (this will help to prevent the peel from rising in the jars).

8 Ladle the marmalade into the warmed, sterilized jars and cover immediately with sterilized lids. Label and store in a cool, dry, dark place. Refrigerate after opening.

Orange & Cardamom Marmalade

With its floral notes, cardamom is a delicious addition to orange marmalade. Serve with warm croissants or brioche for breakfast.

20 cardamom pods
2 pounds, 4 ounces oranges

2 lemons
10 cups granulated sugar

MAKES ABOUT: 6 pounds, 8 ounces (10 cups) PREPARATION TIME: 50 minutes, plus 15 minutes cooling COOKING TIME: 1¾ to 2¼ hours

1 Put the cardamom pods in a mortar and pestle and bash to crack the pods. Alternatively, use a wooden rolling pin. Tie in a double thickness of cheesecloth.

2 Cut the oranges and lemons in half and squeeze out the juice and seeds. Tie the seeds, and any extra membrane that has come away during squeezing, in another piece of cheesecloth.

3 Either by hand or using the shredding attachment of a food processor, slice the orange and lemon peel, with its pith, into thin shreds.

4 Put the orange and lemon juice and peel, cheesecloth bags and 10 cups water in a preserving pan and slowly bring to a boil. Reduce the heat and simmer gently 1½ to 2 hours until the peel is very soft and the liquid reduced by about half. Stir from time to time to prevent the mixture from sticking to the bottom of the pan.

5 Remove the cheesecloth bags from the pan and let cool 5 minutes before squeezing them well and allowing the juice to run back into the pan. Discard the bags.

6 Add the sugar to the pan and stir until completely dissolved. Bring to a boil and boil rapidly about 15 minutes, or until setting point is reached. Test for a set either with a candy thermometer (it should read 221°F) or put a teaspoon of the marmalade onto a cold saucer and let cool a few minutes. If it wrinkles when you push it with your finger, then it is ready to use.

7 Meanwhile, sterilize enough jars in the oven so that they are ready to use (see page 14).

8 Remove the pan from the heat and skim with a slotted spoon to remove any scum. Let cool 15 minutes (this will help to prevent the peel from rising in the jars).

9 Ladle the marmalade into the warmed, sterilized jars and cover immediately with sterilized lids. Label and store in a cool, dry, dark place. Refrigerate after opening.

Chunky Scotch Marmalade

A delicious combination that makes an excellent gift for Scotch lovers. The recipe also works well with rum or brandy.

2 pounds, 4 ounces Seville oranges (bitter oranges)
juice of 2 lemons

10 cups granulated sugar
⅓ cup Scotch whisky

MAKES ABOUT: 6 pounds, 8 ounces (10 cups)   PREPARATION TIME: 45 minutes, plus 15 minutes cooling
COOKING TIME: 2¼ hours

1 Cut the oranges in half and squeeze out the juice and seeds. Tie the seeds, and any extra membrane that has come away during squeezing, in a piece of cheesecloth.

2 Either by hand or using the shredding attachment of a food processor, slice the orange peel, with its pith, into thick, chunky shreds.

3 Put the orange juice and peel, lemon juice, cheesecloth bag and 10 cups water in a preserving pan and slowly bring to a boil. Reduce the heat and simmer gently about 2 hours until the peel is really soft and the liquid reduced by about half.

4 Remove the cheesecloth bag from the pan and let cool 5 minutes before squeezing it well and allowing the juice to run back into the pan. Discard the bag.

5 Add the sugar to the pan and stir until completely dissolved. Bring to a boil and boil rapidly about

15 minutes, or until setting point is reached. Test for a set either with a candy thermometer (it should read 221°F) or put a teaspoon of the marmalade onto a cold saucer and let cool a few minutes. If it wrinkles when you push it with your finger, then it is ready to use.

6 Meanwhile, sterilize enough jars in the oven so that they are ready to use (see page 14).

7 Remove the pan from the heat and skim with a slotted spoon to remove any scum. Stir in the Scotch. Let cool 15 minutes (this will help to prevent the peel from rising in the jars).

8 Ladle the marmalade into the warmed, sterilized jars and cover immediately with sterilized lids. Label and store in a cool, dry, dark place. Refrigerate after opening.

Emma's tip If you like a dark, traditional marmalade, add 2 tablespoons treacle (or molasses), or replace ½ cup of the granulated sugar with dark brown sugar.

Jellies
& Curds

Elderberry Jelly

To make this preserve you will need to gather wild elderberries in early to mid autumn when they are in season. Serve with roast meat dishes or try spooned on top of stewed apples. It is also lovely used to fill a Victoria sponge cake.

2 pounds, 4 ounces (8 to 8½ cups) elderberries
2 pounds, 4 ounces cooking apples

1 cup granulated sugar per 1 cup extract

MAKES ABOUT: 6 x 8-ounce jars PREPARATION TIME: 40 minutes, plus 24 hours straining
COOKING TIME: 1 hour 20 minutes

1 Remove any large stalks and the leaves from the elderberries. Without peeling or coring, roughly chop the apples into thick chunks, discarding any bruised or damaged pieces.

2 Put the elderberries and apples in a preserving pan and add 5 cups water. Bring to a boil, then reduce the heat and simmer 45 to 60 minutes until the fruits are soft and pulpy. Stir from time to time, to prevent the mixture from sticking to the bottom of the pan.

3 Meanwhile, prepare a scalded jelly bag or clean lint-free dish towel, attached to the legs of an upturned stool, with a large bowl underneath.

4 Pour the mixture into the bag (or towel) and let it drip into the bowl overnight or at least 24 hours. Don't be tempted to push the pulp through the bag or the jelly will be cloudy.

5 The next day, discard the pulp and measure the extract. Pour the extract into a preserving pan and for every 1 cup of extract, add 1 cup sugar.

6 Meanwhile, sterilize enough jars in the oven so that they are ready to use (see page 14).

7 Gently heat the mixture, stirring all the time, until the sugar has dissolved. Bring to a boil and boil rapidly about 10 minutes until setting point is reached. Test for a set either with a candy thermometer (it should read 221°F) or put a teaspoon of the jelly onto a cold saucer and let cool a few minutes. If it wrinkles when you push it with your finger, then it is ready to use.

8 Remove the pan from the heat and skim with a slotted spoon to remove any scum.

9 Ladle the jelly into the warmed, sterilized jars and cover immediately with sterilized lids. Label and store in a cool, dry, dark place. Refrigerate after opening.

Crab Apple Jelly

Crab apples are not available to buy commercially but you may have them growing in the garden or find them growing wild in parks and woodland. They make a pretty pink jelly that is particularly good served with roast pork or beef.

3 pounds, 2 ounces crab apples
5 cloves or 2 star anise (optional)

1 cup granulated sugar per 1 cup extract

MAKES ABOUT: 6 x 8-ounce jars   PREPARATION TIME: 1¼ hours, plus 24 hours straining
COOKING TIME: 1 hour 50 minutes

1 Without peeling or coring, cut the crab apples into quarters, discarding any bruised or damaged pieces.

2 Put the chopped apples in a preserving pan and add enough water to cover them. If you like, add the cloves or star anise for added flavor. Bring to a boil, then reduce the heat and simmer gently about 1½ hours until the crab apples are soft. Stir from time to time to prevent the mixture from sticking to the bottom of the pan.

3 Meanwhile, prepare a scalded jelly bag or clean lint-free dish towel, attached to the legs of an upturned stool, with a large bowl underneath.

4 Pour the mixture into the bag (or towel) and let it drip into the bowl overnight or at least 24 hours. Don't be tempted to push the pulp through the bag or the jelly will be cloudy.

5 The next day, discard the pulp and measure the extract. Pour the extract into a preserving pan and for every cup of extract, add 1 cup sugar.

6 Meanwhile, sterilize enough jars in the oven so that they are ready to use (see page 14).

7 Remove the pan from the heat and skim with a slotted spoon to remove any scum.

8 Heat gently, stirring all the time, until the sugar has dissolved. Bring to a boil and boil rapidly about 10 minutes until setting point is reached. Test for a set either with a candy thermometer (it should read 221°F) or put a teaspoon of the jelly onto a cold saucer and let cool a few minutes. If it wrinkles when you push it with your finger, then it is ready to use.

9 Ladle the jelly into the warmed, sterilized jars and cover immediately with sterilized lids. Label and store in a cool, dry, dark place. Refrigerate after opening.

Mint Jelly

This is a fresh and tangy jelly to accompany roast lamb or sausages. You can also add it to salad dressings for a Moroccan twist. Make sage and rosemary jelly in the same way.

3 pounds, 5 ounces cooking apples
2 large mint sprigs plus 6 tablespoons chopped
   mint leaves

3⅓ cups distilled white vinegar
1 cup granulated sugar per 1 cup extract
green paste food coloring (optional)

MAKES ABOUT: 6 x 8-ounce jars   PREPARATION TIME: 35 minutes, plus 24 hours straining
COOKING TIME: 1 hour 15 minutes

1 Without peeling or coring, chop the apples into thick chunks, discarding any bruised or damaged pieces.

2 Put the chopped apples in a preserving pan and add 3⅓ cups water and the mint sprigs. Bring to a boil, then reduce the heat and simmer about 1 hour until the apples are soft and pulpy. Stir from time to time to prevent the mixture from sticking to the bottom of the pan.

3 Add the vinegar, return to a boil and boil for 5 minutes.

4 Meanwhile, prepare a scalded jelly bag or clean lint-free dish towel, attached to the legs of an upturned stool, with a large bowl underneath.

5 Pour the mixture into the bag (or towel) and let it drip into the bowl overnight or at least 24 hours. Don't be tempted to push the pulp through the bag or the jelly will be cloudy.

6 The next day, discard the pulp and measure the extract. Pour the extract into a preserving pan and for every cup of extract, add 1 cup sugar.

7 Meanwhile, sterilize enough jars in the oven so that they are ready to use (see page 14).

8 Gently heat the mixture, stirring all the time, until the sugar has dissolved. Bring to a boil and boil rapidly for about 10 minutes until setting point is reached. Test for a set either with a candy thermometer (it should read 221°F) or put a teaspoon of the jelly onto a cold saucer and let cool a few minutes. If it wrinkles when you push it with your finger, then it is ready to use.

9 Remove the pan from the heat and skim with a slotted spoon to remove any scum. Stir in the chopped mint and color the mixture a shade of green by adding a tiny drop of food coloring, if using.

10 Ladle the jelly into the warmed, sterilized jars and cover immediately with sterilized lids. Label and store in a cool, dry, dark place. Refrigerate after opening.

Hot Chili Jelly

This is for those who like something hot and fiery with cold meats, sausages or burgers. One of the staff at Bay Tree recommends this jelly eaten with plain yogurt.

2 pounds, 4 ounces cooking apples
9 to 10 red chilies, finely chopped

2 cups red wine vinegar
1 cup granulated sugar per 1 cup of extract

MAKES ABOUT: 4 x 8-ounce jars PREPARATION TIME: 45 minutes, plus 24 hours straining and 10 minutes cooling COOKING TIME: 1 hour 10 minutes

1 Without peeling or coring, roughly chop the apples into thick, medium chunks, discarding any bruised or damaged pieces.

2 Put the chopped apples in a preserving pan and add 2¼ cups water and 6 of the chopped chilies, with their seeds. Bring to a boil, then reduce the heat and simmer about 45 minutes until the apples are soft and pulpy. Stir from time to time to prevent the mixture from sticking to the bottom of the pan.

3 Add the vinegar, return to a boil and boil for 5 minutes.

4 Meanwhile, prepare a scalded jelly bag or clean lint-free dish towel, attached to the legs of an upturned stool, with a large bowl underneath.

5 Pour the mixture into the bag (or towel) and let it drip into the bowl overnight or at least 24 hours. Don't be tempted to push the pulp through the bag or the jelly will be cloudy.

6 The next day, discard the pulp and measure the extract. Pour the extract into a preserving pan and for every cup of extract, add 1 cup sugar.

7 Meanwhile, sterilize enough jars in the oven so that they are ready to use (see page 14).

8 Gently heat the mixture, stirring all the time, until the sugar has dissolved. Bring to a boil and boil rapidly about 10 minutes until setting point is reached. Test for a set either with a candy thermometer (it should read 221°F) or put a teaspoon of the jelly onto a cold saucer and let cool a few minutes. If it wrinkles when you push it with your finger, then it is ready to use.

9 Remove the pan from the heat and skim with a slotted spoon to remove any scum. Stir in the remaining chilies, without the seeds. Let the jelly cool 10 minutes (this will help to prevent the chili from rising in the jars).

10 Ladle the jelly into the warmed, sterilized jars and cover immediately with sterilized lids. Label and store in a cool, dry, dark place. Refrigerate after opening.

Black Pepper & Cumin Jelly

Serve this jelly with soft cheese or cold meats, or alternatively use as an ingredient in stews, gravies and stir-fries, or as a glaze on grilled meats.

2 pounds, 4 ounces cooking apples
2 tablespoons black peppercorns, lightly crushed
2 tablespoons cumin seeds, lightly crushed

2 cups cider vinegar
1 cup granulated sugar per 1 cup of extract

MAKES ABOUT: 4 x 8-ounce jars PREPARATION TIME: 50 minutes, plus 24 hours straining and 10 minutes cooling COOKING TIME: 1 hour 10 minutes

1 Without peeling or coring, roughly chop the apples into thick, medium chunks, discarding any bruised or damaged pieces.

2 Put the chopped apples in a preserving pan and add 2¼ cups water, 1 tablespoon of the peppercorns and 1 tablespoon of the cumin seeds. Bring to a boil, then reduce the heat and simmer about 45 minutes until the apples are soft and pulpy. Stir from time to time to prevent the mixture from sticking to the bottom of the pan.

3 Add the vinegar, return to a boil and boil for 5 minutes.

4 Meanwhile, prepare a scalded jelly bag or clean lint-free dish towel, attached to the legs of an upturned stool, with a large bowl underneath.

5 Pour the mixture into the bag (or towel) and let it drip into the bowl overnight or at least 24 hours. Don't be tempted to push the pulp through the bag or the jelly will be cloudy.

6 The next day, discard the pulp and measure the extract. Pour the extract into a preserving pan and for every cup of extract, add 1 cup sugar.

7 Meanwhile, sterilize enough jars in the oven so that they are ready to use (see page 14).

8 Gently heat the mixture, stirring all the time, until the sugar has dissolved. Bring to a boil and boil rapidly about 10 minutes until setting point is reached. Test for a set either with a candy thermometer (it should read 221°F) or put a teaspoon of the jelly onto a cold saucer and let cool a few minutes. If it wrinkles when you push it with your finger, then it is ready to use.

9 Remove the pan from the heat and skim with a slotted spoon to remove any scum. Stir in the remaining peppercorns and cumin seeds. Let the jelly cool 10 minutes (this will help to prevent the spices from rising in the jars).

10 Ladle the jelly into the warmed, sterilized jars and cover immediately with sterilized lids. Label and store in a cool, dry, dark place. Refrigerate after opening.

Passion Fruit Curd

Intensely scented, this is passion fruit captured in a jar. For a delicious, super-quick dessert, serve a large spoonful of this curd on top of Greek yogurt and add a generous sprinkling of blueberries.

6 passion fruits
3½ tablespoons unsalted butter, cut into
  small pieces

heaped ½ cup granulated sugar
2 large eggs

MAKES ABOUT: 1 pound, 5 ounces (2 cups) PREPARATION TIME: 30 minutes
COOKING TIME: 25 minutes

1 Cut the passion fruits in half and scoop out the flesh into a strainer set in a bowl. Using a wooden spoon, push the flesh into the bowl. Reserve 1 tablespoon of the seeds and discard the rest.

2 Sterilize enough small jars in the oven so that they are ready to use (see page 14).

3 Put the passion fruit juice, butter and sugar in the top of a double boiler. Set over gently simmering water. Stir the mixture until the sugar has dissolved and the butter has melted.

4 Break the eggs into a bowl and, using a balloon whisk, beat together well. Whisk the eggs into the butter mixture.

5 Heat gently and cook about 20 minutes, whisking frequently, until the mixture is thick enough to coat the back of a wooden spoon. Do not let the mixture boil or it will curdle. If the curd does start to split, remove from the heat and whisk vigorously until smooth.

6 Stir in the reserved passion fruit seeds to add crunch and color to the curd.

7 Pour the curd into the warmed, sterilized jars. Cover immediately with sterilized lids. Let cool completely before storing in the refrigerator up to 2 weeks. Once opened, eat within 3 days.

Emma's tip As with all curds, you have to be patient when making this recipe. Don't be tempted to turn the heat up too high or the mixture might curdle. You will need to whisk until the mixture is thick; this can take from 20 to 40 minutes.

Very Lemon Curd

The title describes this curd perfectly. Packed with lemon zest, it is ideal for spreading thickly on toast or crumpets, or use as a filling for a cake or a lemon tart. And who can resist devouring it right from the jar?

grated zest and juice of 4 lemons
¾ cup (1½ sticks) unsalted butter, cut into
  small pieces

1⅓ cups granulated sugar
4 large eggs

MAKES ABOUT: 1 pound, 12 ounces (2½ to 3 cups) PREPARATION TIME: 30 minutes
COOKING TIME: 25 minutes

1 Sterilize enough small jars in the oven so that they are ready to use (see page 14).

2 Strain the lemon juice into the top of a double boiler. Set over gently simmering water.

3 Add the lemon zest, butter and sugar and heat gently, stirring the mixture until the sugar has dissolved and the butter has melted.

4 Break the eggs into a bowl and, using a balloon whisk, beat together well. Whisk the eggs into the butter mixture.

5 Heat gently and cook about 20 minutes, whisking frequently, until the mixture is thick enough to coat the back of a wooden spoon. Do not let the mixture boil or it will curdle. If the curd does start to split, remove from the heat and whisk vigorously until smooth.

6 Pour the curd into the warmed, sterilized jars. Cover immediately with sterilized lids. Let cool completely before storing in the refrigerator up to 2 weeks. Once opened, eat within 3 days.

Emma's tip To make Lime Curd, replace the lemons with the zest and juice from 6 limes. You could also try a mixture of lemons and limes together.

Raspberry Curd

Serve this luxurious, buttery curd spread on toast or use it to sandwich a chocolate or vanilla layer cake together. You can use blackberries instead of raspberries and use in the same way. Both will also be delicious when used to fill a tart, as a change from lemon curd.

1 pound, 5 ounces (about 2¼ to 2½ cups) raspberries
1 tablespoon orange juice

⅔ cup unsalted butter, cut into small pieces
1¼ cups granulated sugar
4 large eggs

MAKES ABOUT: 1 pound, 8 ounces (2¼ to 2½ cups)   PREPARATION TIME: 40 minutes
COOKING TIME: 30 minutes

1 Sterilize enough small jars in the oven so that they are ready to use (see page 14).

2 Put the raspberries and orange juice in a pot. Heat gently and simmer for 5 minutes until the juices start to run and the fruit is very soft.

3 Using the back of a wooden spoon, push the cooked raspberries through a strainer into the top of a double boiler. Set over gently simmering water.

4 Add the butter and sugar to the top of the double boiler and heat gently, stirring the mixture until the sugar has dissolved and the butter has melted.

5 Break the eggs into a bowl and, using a balloon whisk, beat together well. Whisk the eggs into the butter mixture.

6 Heat gently and cook about 20 minutes, whisking frequently, until the mixture is thick enough to coat the back of a wooden spoon. Do not let the mixture boil or it will curdle. If the curd does start to split, remove from the heat and whisk vigorously until smooth.

7 Pour the curd into the warmed, sterilized jars. Cover immediately with sterilized lids. Let cool completely before storing in the refrigerator up to 2 weeks. Once opened, eat within 3 days.

Tangerine Curd

A twist on traditional lemon curd, this curd is still rich but has a sweeter flavor. It is delicious when used to fill pastries, or spread on toast, scones or muffins. An alternative to tangerines are clementines (sometimes called seedless tangerines) or satsumas, which are various types of mandarins varying in their sweetness. Oranges, too, can be used. Whichever fruit you choose, don't expect the curd to be bright orange, as the color of the curd comes from the egg yolks rather than the fruit juice.

grated zest and juice of 4 tangerines
½ cup plus 1 tablespoon unsalted butter, cut into small pieces

1 cup granulated sugar
3 large eggs

MAKES ABOUT: 1 pound, 6 ounces (2 to 2½ cups) PREPARATION TIME: 30 minutes
COOKING TIME: 25 minutes

1 Sterilize enough small jars in the oven so that they are ready to use (see page 14).

2 Strain the tangerine juice into the top of a double boiler set over gently simmering water.

3 Add the tangerine zest, butter and sugar to the top of the double boiler and heat gently, stirring the mixture until the sugar has dissolved and the butter has melted.

4 Break the eggs into a bowl and, using a balloon whisk, beat together well. Whisk the eggs into the butter mixture.

5 Heat gently and cook about 20 minutes, whisking frequently, until the mixture is thick enough to coat the back of a wooden spoon. Do not let the mixture boil or it will curdle. If the curd does start to split, remove from the heat and whisk vigorously until smooth.

6 Pour the curd into the warmed, sterilized jars. Cover immediately with sterilized lids. Let cool completely before storing in the refrigerator up to 2 weeks. Once opened, eat within 3 days.

Emma's tip If you prefer a very tangy flavor to your curd, replace 1 tangerine with the grated zest and juice of 1 lemon, which cuts through the sweetness of the tangerine.

Coconut Curd

A popular preserve in Malaysia, Singapore and Indonesia is Kaya, also known as Coconut Curd or Coconut Egg Jam. Similar to a curd, the authentic product uses fresh screwpine (pandan) leaves, which have a pine and citrus taste. As these can usually only be found in Asian markets, the recipe includes them as optional—it is delicious with or without them. It is served as a snack spread on buttered toast.

scant 1 cup coconut milk
¼ cup palm sugar
¼ cup granulated sugar

4 fresh screwpine (pandan) leaves (optional)
4 large eggs

MAKES ABOUT: 10 ounces (1 cup)   PREPARATION TIME: 20 minutes   COOKING TIME: 25 minutes

1 Sterilize enough small jars in the oven so that they are ready to use (see page 14).

2 Put the coconut milk, palm and granulated sugars, and screwpine leaves, if using, in the top of a double boiler set over gently simmering water. Stir the mixture until the sugar has dissolved.

3 Break the eggs into a bowl and, using a balloon whisk, beat together well. Whisk the eggs into the coconut mixture.

4 Heat gently and cook about 20 minutes, whisking frequently, until the mixture is thick enough to coat the back of a wooden spoon. Do not let the mixture boil or it will curdle. If the curd does start to split, remove from the heat and whisk vigorously until smooth.

5 Remove the screwpine leaves, if you have used them.

6 Pour the curd into the warmed, sterilized jars. Cover immediately with sterilized lids. Let cool completely before storing in the refrigerator up to 2 weeks. Once opened, eat within 3 days.

Very Ginger Curd

Packed with fresh and preserved ginger, just the smell of this luxurious curd will make you reach for a spoon! It is perfect on toast or crumpets, or use to sandwich together ginger snaps.

juice of 2 lemons
1¾ ounces (a heaped ⅓ cup) ginger root, peeled and grated
3 tablespoons medium-dry white wine
½ cup minus 1 tablespoon unsalted butter, cut into small pieces

1½ cups granulated sugar
4 large eggs
2 ounces preserved ginger (about 3 to 4 balls), finely chopped

MAKES ABOUT: 1 pound, 8 ounces (2¼ to 2½ cups) PREPARATION TIME: 30 minutes
COOKING TIME: 25 minutes

1 Sterilize enough small jars in the oven so that they are ready to use (see page 14).

2 Strain the lemon juice into the top of a double boiler set over gently simmering water.

3 Add the grated ginger, wine, butter and sugar to the top of the double boiler and heat gently, stirring the mixture until the sugar has dissolved and the butter has melted.

4 Break the eggs into a bowl and, using a balloon whisk, beat together well. Whisk the eggs into the butter mixture.

5 Heat gently and cook about 20 minutes, whisking frequently, until the mixture is thick enough to coat the back of a wooden spoon. Do not let the mixture boil or it will curdle. If the curd does start to split, remove from the heat and whisk vigorously until smooth.

6 Stir the preserved ginger into the mixture.

7 Pour the curd into the warmed, sterilized jars. Cover immediately with sterilized lids. Let cool completely before storing in the refrigerator up to 2 weeks. Once opened, eat within 3 days.

Emma's tip Store ginger root in the freezer rather than the refrigerator so that you always have a fresh piece when needed. When you come to use it, simply grate as much as you need. It is not even necessary to thaw it first.

Lé Nièr Beurre

Black Butter, a traditional delicacy from Jersey in the Channel Islands off France, was usually made in the fall, when groups of men and children would gather the apples while the women peeled them. It is rich, spicy and dark, as its name suggests. Serve it spread on fresh bread or as an accompaniment to cold meats.

4¼ cups cider
3 pounds eating apples, peeled, cored and sliced
grated zest and juice of 1 lemon
1½-inch piece of licorice stick, very finely chopped

1¾ cups granulated sugar per 2½ cups of puree
2 teaspoons ground cinnamon
1 teaspoon ground allspice
½ teaspoon ground cloves

MAKES ABOUT: 4 pounds, 3 ounces (6½ to 7 cups) PREPARATION TIME: 30 minutes
COOKING TIME: 2 hours

1 Pour the cider into a large, heavy pot, bring to a boil and boil rapidly about 20 minutes until reduced by half.

2 Add the apple slices and simmer about 40 minutes until the apples are soft and pulpy. Stir from time to time to prevent the mixture from sticking to the bottom of the pan.

3 Add the lemon zest and juice and licorice and continue to cook 5 minutes until the mixture is well reduced and there is no excess liquid in the pot.

4 Measure the puree and return it to the cleaned pot. For each 2½ cups of puree add 1¾ cups sugar. Add the cinnamon, allspice and cloves.

5 Heat gently, stirring all the time, until the sugar has dissolved. Continue cooking about 1 hour until the mixture is a thick spreading consistency. Stir frequently and keep the heat low since the mixture tends to spit.

6 Meanwhile, sterilize enough small jars in the oven so that they are ready to use (see page 14).

7 Pour the butter into the warmed, sterilized jars and cover immediately with sterilized lids. Label and store in a cool, dry, dark place at least 3 months before eating, to let the butter mature and darken. Refrigerate after opening.

Apricot & Orange Butter

Fresh apricots combine beautifully with oranges. Serve this butter spread thickly on croissants, buttery brioche, coarse wholewheat toast or pancakes for a delicious breakfast. You will be tempted to eat several of whatever you choose!

2 pounds, 4 ounces apricots, pitted
grated zest and juice of 2 oranges

1¾ cups granulated sugar per 2½ cups of puree

MAKES ABOUT: 2 pounds, 4 ounces (3½ cups)   PREPARATION TIME: 30 minutes
COOKING TIME: 1 hour 35 minutes

1 Put the apricots in a large pot and add 1¼ cups water. Bring to a boil, then reduce the heat and simmer gently about 45 minutes until the apricots are soft and pulpy.

2 Using a wooden spoon, push the mixture through a strainer into a large bowl.

3 Measure the puree and return it to the cleaned pot. For each 2½ cups of puree add 1¾ cups sugar.

4 Heat gently, stirring all the time, until the sugar has dissolved. Bring to a boil and boil rapidly

30 to 40 minutes until the mixture is a thick spreading consistency. Stir frequently to prevent the mixture from sticking to the bottom of the pot.

5 Meanwhile, sterilize enough small jars in the oven so that they are ready to use (see page 14).

6 Pour the butter into the warmed, sterilized jars and cover immediately with sterilized lids. Label and store in a cool, dry, dark place. Refrigerate after opening.

Emma's tip Fruit butters and cheeses are easy to make but pureeing the fruit can be hard work. To help speed matters up, crush the fruit with a potato masher or fork when it's soft and then push it through the strainer in small batches.

Damson Cheese

A lovely way to use a glut of British damson plums, this cheese can also be made with any small plums you have. You can make Apple Cheese in the same way by replacing the damsons with apples and the allspice with ½ teaspoon ground cinnamon and ¼ teaspoon ground cloves. Alternatively, use a mixture of half apples and half blackberries for a stunning, dark Bramble Cheese. All can be served with cheese, pâtés, cold meats or roast pork.

2 pounds, 4 ounces damson plums
1 cup granulated sugar per 1 cup of puree

½ teaspoon ground allspice
mild-flavored olive oil or glycerin, for brushing

MAKES ABOUT: 2 pounds, 4 ounces (3½ cups) PREPARATION TIME: 25 minutes
COOKING TIME: 1 hour 10 minutes

1 Put the damson plums in a large, heavy pot and add enough water to just cover the fruit. Bring to a boil, then reduce the heat and simmer gently about 20 minutes until the plums are soft. Scoop out the pits with a slotted spoon as they rise to the surface.

2 Using a wooden spoon, push the mixture through a strainer into a large bowl.

3 Measure the puree and return it to the cleaned pot. For every cup of puree add 1 cup sugar. Add the allspice.

4 Heat gently, stirring all the time, until the sugar has dissolved. Bring to a boil and boil rapidly 30 to 40 minutes until the mixture is a thick spreading consistency. Stir frequently to prevent the mixture from sticking to the bottom of the pan. The cheese is ready when a wooden spoon drawn across the bottom of the pot reveals the bottom cleanly.

5 Meanwhile, brush the insides of a small bowl or small, straight-sided individual molds or ramekins with a little olive oil.

6 Spoon the cheese into the prepared dishes and level the surface. Cut out circles of wax paper and lightly press them onto the tops of the cheese. Then cover the tops of the dishes in plastic wrap.

7 Store the cheese in the refrigerator at least 1 month before eating, to allow the cheese to mature.

8 To serve, turn the cheese out of its dish and serve whole, sliced into small portions. Eat within 1 year.

Emma's tip Like all fruit cheeses, this is extremely good served with a cheeseboard, but an alternative way of serving is to cut it into cubes, lightly sprinkle with granulated sugar and eat just as it is!

Membrillo

This traditional quince cheese is known as membrillo in Spain, marmelado in Portugal and pâté de Coings in France. In the 13th century, fruit cheeses were known as "marmalades," which is the Portuguese word for quince. Serve Membrillo with a single cheese such as Manchego (a hard Spanish cheese) or as part of a cheeseboard.

2 pounds, 4 ounces quinces
1 cup granulated sugar per 1 cup of puree
mild-flavored olive oil or glycerin, for brushing

MAKES ABOUT: 2 pounds, 4 ounces (3½ cups)   PREPARATION TIME: 35 minutes
COOKING TIME: 1 hour 20 minutes

1 Without peeling or coring, chop the quinces, discarding any bruised or damaged pieces.

2 Put the chopped quinces in a large, heavy pot and add 1¼ cups water to just cover the fruit. Bring to a boil, then reduce the heat and simmer gently about 30 minutes until the quinces are soft and pulpy. Stir from time to time to prevent the mixture from sticking to the bottom of the pot.

3 Using a wooden spoon, push the mixture through a strainer into a large bowl.

4 Measure the puree and return it to the cleaned pot. For every cup of puree add 1 cup sugar.

5 Heat gently, stirring all the time, until the sugar has dissolved. Bring to a boil and boil rapidly 30 to 40 minutes until the mixture is a thick spreading consistency. Stir frequently to prevent the mixture from sticking to the bottom of the pot. The cheese is ready when a wooden spoon drawn across the bottom of the pot reveals the bottom cleanly.

6 Meanwhile, brush the insides of a small bowl or small, straight-sided individual molds or ramekins with a little olive oil.

7 Spoon the cheese into the prepared dishes and level the surface. Cut out circles of wax paper and lightly press them onto the tops of the cheese. Then cover the tops of the dishes in plastic wrap.

8 Store the cheese in the refrigerator at least 1 month before eating, to allow the cheese to mature.

9 To serve, turn the cheese out of its dish and serve whole, sliced into small portions. Eat within 1 year.

Conserved
& Bottled

Snapdragon

You may wonder how this conserve came to have its name but I don't know! It is probably because of the game Snapdragon (see below). We like to eat it right from the jar with a long fork at Christmas time, or as a winter fruit salad.

1 cup rum
1¾ cups dried apricots
2 cups dried figs
2 cups raisins
1¼ cups granulated sugar

grated zest and juice of 1 lemon
grated zest and juice of 1 orange
½ cup blanched almonds

MAKES ABOUT: 3 pounds, 5 ounces (5 cups)   PREPARATION TIME: 20 minutes
COOKING TIME: 10 minutes

1 Sterilize enough jars in the oven so that they are ready to use (see page 14).

2 Put the rum and ¾ cup water in a large, heavy pot. Add all the remaining ingredients, except the almonds.

3 Cover the pan and slowly bring to a boil. Stir the ingredients together well, reduce the heat and simmer 5 minutes.

4 Remove the pan from the heat and half-fill the warmed, sterilized jars with the conserve. Using about 15 almonds for each jar, arrange the almonds in a layer on top of the conserve and then top with the remaining conserve to fill the jars.

5 Cover immediately with sterilized lids. Label and store in a cool, dry, dark place. Refrigerate after opening.

Emma's tip If you wish to find your true love, you could play the game Snapdragon. Also known as Flapdragon, this Victorian parlor game involved raisins being snatched from a bowl of burning brandy and eaten, at the risk of burning mouths. The traditional belief was that the person who snatched the most fruits would meet their true love within the year. The game was played in England, the United States and Canada during the winter months, particularly at Christmas and Halloween.

Strawberry Conserve

This soft-set, whole strawberry conserve is best served spooned, rather than spread. It is delicious served on top of meringues, or on warm scones with a large spoonful of thick clotted cream (or whipped cream).

2 pounds, 4 ounces small strawberries
5 cups granulated sugar

juice of 2 lemons

MAKES ABOUT: 2 pounds, 4 ounces (3½ cups)   PREPARATION TIME: 15 minutes, plus 48 hours macerating and 15 minutes cooling   COOKING TIME: 20 minutes

1 In a large bowl, put the strawberries and sugar in layers. Cover and let macerate at room temperature 24 hours.

2 The next day, put the mixture in a pot, slowly bring to a boil, stirring until the sugar dissolves, then boil 5 minutes until the strawberries have softened but not broken up.

3 Return the mixture to the bowl, cover and leave it at room temperature for another 24 hours.

4 Sterilize enough jars in the oven so that they are ready to use (see page 14).

5 Return the mixture to the pot and add the lemon juice. Bring to a boil, then boil 5 to 10 minutes until setting point is reached. Test for a set either with a candy thermometer (it should read 221°F) or put a teaspoon of the conserve onto a cold saucer and leave it until completely cool, a few minutes. If it wrinkles when you push it with your finger, then it is ready to use.

6 Remove the pot from the heat and let cool 15 minutes (this will help to prevent the strawberries from rising in the jars).

7 Ladle the conserve into the warmed, sterilized jars. Cover immediately with sterilized lids. Label and store in a cool, dry, dark place. Eat within 3 months and refrigerate after opening.

Emma's tip Leaving the strawberries in sugar helps to draw out their juices and keeps them whole during cooking. It is important to use small, juicy whole strawberries, when they are in season.

Bar-le-Duc

This red currant conserve originated from Bar-le-Duc in the Lorraine region of France. In the authentic recipe, the seeds of the currants are removed but it is just as delicious if this time-consuming task is not done. Serve it on thin toast or, as they do in France, with madeleine cakes or as the dessert known as Duchesse-le-Duc. This is scoops of vanilla ice cream, surrounded by a skirt of Bar-le-Duc, served with sweetened whipped cream and decorated with sugar violets.

1 pound, 2 ounces (heaped 4 cups) red currants, stripped

3¾ cups granulated sugar

MAKES ABOUT: 2 pounds, 12 ounces (4 to 4½ cups) PREPARATION TIME: 20 minutes, plus 24 hours macerating and 30 minutes cooling COOKING TIME: 5 minutes

1 Put the red currants in a bowl, add the sugar and stir together. Cover and let macerate at room temperature 24 hours.

2 The next day, put the mixture in a pot, slowly bring to a boil and boil 3 minutes. Remove the pot from the heat and let cool 30 minutes until a skin starts to form.

3 Meanwhile, sterilize enough jars in the oven so that they are ready to use (see page 14).

4 Gently stir the mixture to evenly distribute the red currants, then ladle the conserve into the warmed, sterilized jars. Cover immediately with sterilized lids. Label and store in a cool, dry, dark place. Eat within 3 months and refrigerate after opening.

Emma's tip It is not essential to seed red currants, but if you have time prick each red currant with a sewing needle to help them remain plump during cooking.

Raspberry & Kirsch Conserve

Whole raspberries, suspended in a kirsch syrup, are the perfect preserve to have tucked away to serve at a moment's notice. Add a spoonful to vanilla ice cream, Greek yogurt or fromage frais for an instant dessert.

2 pounds, 4 ounces (8 cups) raspberries
5 cups granulated sugar

2 tablespoons kirsch

MAKES ABOUT: 2 pounds, 4 ounces (3½ cups) PREPARATION TIME: 20 minutes, plus 1 hour 20 minutes standing COOKING TIME: 15 minutes

1 Preheat the oven to 350°F.

2 Put the raspberries on a baking tray in a single layer. Sprinkle the sugar on a separate baking tray. Bake both trays 15 minutes.

3 Tip the raspberries and sugar into a large bowl and gently stir together until combined. Let stand 20 minutes. Repeat the stirring and standing three more times.

4 Meanwhile, sterilize enough jars in the oven so that they are ready to use (see page 14).

5 Stir the kirsch into the raspberry mixture.

6 Ladle the conserve into the warmed, sterilized jars. Cover immediately with sterilized lids. Label and store in a cool, dry, dark place. Eat within 3 months and refrigerate after opening.

Emma's tip Kirsch, an abbreviation of its full name Kirschwasser, originated in Germany. It is a clear, colorless fruit brandy made from cherries. It is not sweet (unlike cherry brandies) and has a subtle, sour cherry and almond flavor, which comes from the pits. Kirsch complements raspberries beautifully but other liqueurs such as framboise (made from raspberries), brandy and cherry brandy can be used instead for this recipe.

Apricot & Orange Mincemeat

This luscious mincemeat is packed with plump apricots and orange, with a subtle hint of sherry, too. It makes a delicious change from the usual mincemeat that you buy. Use it to fill mince pies or baked apples.

1¾ cups dried apricots
grated zest and juice of 2 large oranges
1 pound, 10 ounces (5 to 5½ cups)
  mixed dried fruit
heaped ½ cup candied orange peel

1 cup sherry
¼ cup orange marmalade
2½ cups Demerara sugar
2⅓ cups shredded beef or vegetable suet
1 tablespoon ground apple pie spice

MAKES ABOUT: 4 pounds, 8 ounces (7 cups) PREPARATION TIME: 25 minutes, plus 48 hours macerating and 2 weeks maturing

1 Using scissors, cut the apricots into small pieces and put in a large bowl. Add the grated orange zest and juice. Put the dried fruit and candied orange peel in a separate large bowl. Add the sherry. Cover both bowls and let macerate 24 hours.

2 The next day, combine the soaked apricots and dried fruits together. Add the marmalade, sugar, suet and apple pie spice and stir well together. Cover the bowl and leave it another 24 hours.

3 Sterilize enough jars in the oven so that they are ready to use (see page 14).

4 Pack the mincemeat into the warmed, sterilized jars, taking care not to leave any air bubbles. Cover immediately with sterilized lids. Label and store in a cool, dry, dark place.

5 Let mature at least 2 weeks before using. Refrigerate after opening.

Emma's tip Dried apricots come in various shapes and forms. For this recipe, choose natural dried apricots that haven't been presoaked. Dark, dried apricots (dark because they haven't been treated with sulfur dioxide) may not look as attractive but their flavor is much more intense than bland, plumper apricots.

Boozy Cherry & Walnut Mincemeat

Vine fruits that are soaked in sherry for several days make this a heady mixture, and all the more delicious with juicy cherries and crunchy walnuts. Perfect for using in baked apples and mince-meat pies. The longer you let it mature, the better.

9 ounces firm cooking apples, peeled, cored
  and grated
1¾ cups candied cherries, cut in half
1 cup walnuts, roughly chopped
3½ cups mixed dried vine fruit

scant 2 cups Demerara sugar
1 cup shredded beef or vegetable suet
1 teaspoon ground apple pie spice
1¼ cups sherry

MAKES ABOUT: 4 pounds (6 to 6½ cups) PREPARATION TIME: 15 minutes, plus 48 hours macerating and 2 weeks maturing

1 Put all the ingredients in a large bowl and stir well together. Cover the bowl and let macerate 48 hours. Stir the mixture occasionally as you pass by.

2 Sterilize enough jars in the oven so that they are ready to use (see page 14).

3 Pack the mincemeat into the warmed, sterilized jars, taking care not to leave any air bubbles. Cover immediately with sterilized lids. Label and store in a cool, dry, dark place.

4 Let mature at least 2 weeks before using. Refrigerate after opening.

Emma's tip Mincemeat was originally a method of preserving meat in alcohol. By the middle of the 20th century, meat was no longer preserved in this way, and the mince "meat" we know today developed. Beef suet is an ingredient of the past and can appear in traditional recipes. Solid vegetable suet is often used instead now in England, making it suitable for vegetarians, but is not widely available in the US. You can choose to use either in this recipe.

Golden Clementines

Glistening whole clementines not only look stunning packed in a jar but they are wonderful to eat, too. They would be a lovely gift, in which case pack them into a 1-quart canning jar (or two 1-pint jars) so that you have one to keep. Serve them as dessert spooned on top of ice cream, Greek yogurt, crème fraîche or ricotta cheese.

10 clementines

1 cup granulated sugar

MAKES ABOUT: 1 quart PREPARATION TIME: 40 minutes, plus 1 hour soaking, 2 to 3 hours cooling and canning (optional) COOKING TIME: 25 minutes

1 Remove the zest from the clementines, cut into thick strips and put in a small pot. Add ¾ cup water and let soak 1 hour.

2 Sterilize a 1-quart canning jar (or two 1-pint jars) so that it is ready to use (see page 14).

3 Peel the clementines and, using the tip of a sharp knife, remove all the white pith. Take care when doing this so that the clementines will look attractive when preserved.

4 Pack the clementines into the warmed, sterilized jars, arranging them attractively.

5 When the clementine zest has soaked, heat gently and simmer 10 minutes.

6 Strain the liquid into a clean, heavy pot and add the sugar. Heat gently, stirring until the sugar has dissolved. Bring to a boil and boil rapidly 5 to 10 minutes until it turns a pale golden color.

7 Pour the syrup into a heatproof measuring cup and make up to 2 cups with water. Leave it 2 to 3 hours until completely cold.

8 When cold, pour the syrup over the clementines, covering them completely. Leave a ½-inch gap between the top of the liquid and the lid. Tap the jars lightly on the counter to remove any air bubbles. Fit the sterilized rubber band or metal lid and seal the jar. If using a screw-band jar, loosen by a quarter-turn after sealing. Label and store in the refrigerator. Eat within 1 month.

9 If you wish to store the preserve for longer, follow the instructions for canning on page 23.

Emma's tip Clementines are very simple to prepare but it can take some time! Use a sharp knife so you can remove all the white pith so that the fruits look stunning in the jar.

Fresh Figs in Manuka Honey

Manuka honey from New Zealand is reputed to have antibacterial properties. Whether it does or not, its rich, strong flavor complements figs perfectly. Serve this preserve as a dessert with cream or Greek yogurt, or, as they do in Greece, with slices of feta cheese.

1⅓ cups Manuka honey
juice of 2 oranges

10 fresh figs

MAKES ABOUT: 1 quart   PREPARATION TIME: 10 minutes, plus canning (optional)
COOKING TIME: 10 minutes

1 Sterilize a 1-quart canning jar so that it is ready to use (see page 14).

2 Put the honey and 1½ cups water in a heavy pot and heat gently until combined. Bring to a boil and boil 2 minutes. Remove the pan from the heat.

3 Add the orange juice and figs to the pan. Return the pan to the heat, bring to a boil, then reduce the heat and simmer 5 minutes until the figs are just tender.

4 Using a slotted spoon, remove the figs from the pan and pack into the warmed, sterilized jar.

5 Pour the remaining liquid over the figs, covering them completely. Leave a ½-inch gap between the top of the liquid and the lid. Tap the jar lightly on the counter to remove any air bubbles. Fit the sterilized rubber band or metal lid and seal the jar. If using a screw-band jar, loosen by a quarter-turn after sealing. Label and let cool completely before storing in the refrigerator. Eat within 1 month.

6 If you wish to store the preserve for longer, follow the instructions for canning on page 23.

Emma's tip Manuka honey can be expensive but you can use other honeys if you prefer. There are hundreds of varieties to choose from but one from a floral nectar source, such as orange blossom honey, would be a delicious and more affordable alternative.

Tipsy Brandied Fruits

You can choose from a variety of fruits to conserve in brandy, all of which make an excellent dessert. If you want to prepare them as a homemade gift, pack in two smaller canning jars rather than one large one so that you have one to keep.

1 pound, 10 ounces small, firm peaches, apricots or nectarines

2 cups granulated sugar
1 cup brandy

MAKES ABOUT: 1 quart   PREPARATION TIME: 40 minutes, plus 2 to 3 hours cooling, 2 weeks maturing and canning (optional)   COOKING TIME: 30 minutes

1 Bring a large pot of water to a boil. Plunge the fruits individually into the boiling water 1 to 2 minutes until their skins split. Remove from the pot using a slotted spoon and use a sharp knife to gently peel off the skin.

2 Sterilize a 1-quart canning jar (or two 1-pint jars) so that it is ready to use (see page 14).

3 Put ¾ cup of the sugar and 2 cups water in a heavy pot and heat gently, stirring until the sugar has dissolved. Add the fruit and simmer gently 5 minutes, turning, until softened slightly.

4 Using a slotted spoon, remove the fruit from the pot and pack into the warmed, sterilized jars.

5 Add the remaining sugar to the liquid in the pot and heat gently, stirring until dissolved. Bring to a boil

and boil until the temperature reaches 230°F on a candy thermometer. Leave it until completely cold.

6 Measure the cooled syrup and add an equal quantity of brandy, then stir together. Pour the syrup over the fruit, covering it completely. Leave a ½-inch gap between the top of the liquid and the lid. Tap the jar lightly on the counter to remove any air bubbles. Fit the rubber band or metal lid and seal the jar. If using a screw-band jar, loosen by a quarter-turn after sealing. Label and store in the refrigerator.

7 Let mature 2 weeks before eating and use within 1 month.

8 If you wish to store the preserve for longer, follow the instructions for canning on page 23.

Emma's tip Whole fruits look very attractive in jars and make a lovely homemade gift, but sliced fruits take up less space. If you would prefer to use sliced fruit, then cut in half and pit the peaches, apricots or nectarines before putting them in the boiling water.

Cherries in Kirsch

Kirsch is a clear liqueur distilled from cherries and is the perfect choice in which to preserve cherries. Serve it spooned over ice cream or use in a Black Forest cake.

1¼ cups granulated sugar
1 pound, 2 ounces (about 2½ cups) cherries

1 cinnamon stick
about ⅔ cup kirsch

MAKES ABOUT: 1 pint   PREPARATION TIME: 30 minutes, plus 2 to 3 hours cooling, 2 weeks maturing and canning (optional)   COOKING TIME: 15 minutes

1 Put ½ cup of the sugar and 1¼ cups water in a heavy pot and heat gently, stirring until the sugar has dissolved. Add the cherries and cinnamon stick and gently simmer 4 to 5 minutes until softened slightly.

2 Drain the cherries and cinnamon stick, reserving the syrup. Return the syrup to the pot.

3 Add the remaining sugar to the pot and heat gently, stirring until dissolved. Bring to a boil and boil until the temperature reaches 230°F on a candy thermometer. Leave it 2 to 3 hours until completely cold.

4 Sterilize a 1-pint canning jar so that it is ready to use (see page 14).

5 Pack the cherries and cinnamon stick into the warmed, sterilized jar.

6 Measure the cooled syrup and add an equal quantity of kirsch, then stir together. Pour the syrup over the cherries, covering them completely. Leave a ½-inch gap between the top of the liquid and the lid. Tap the jar lightly on the counter to remove any air bubbles. Fit the sterilized rubber band or metal lid and seal the jar. If using a screw-band jar, loosen by a quarter-turn after sealing. Label and store in the refrigerator.

7 Let mature 2 weeks before eating and use within 1 month.

8 If you wish to store the preserve for longer, follow the instructions for canning on page 23.

Emma's tip The pits are left in the cherries to help keep their shape; the pits also impart a pleasant almond flavor to the preserve. However, if you would prefer not to include them, use a sharp knife or a cherry pitter to pit the cherries before cooking.

Apricots & Chestnuts in Rum

This is a preserve to make during the chestnut season in fall. Choose plump, smooth nuts as wrinkled ones have a bitter flavor. Serve as a dessert with cream or spoon onto meringues and top with thick cream.

12 ounces (2 cups) shelled fresh chestnuts
12 ounces (2 to 2¼ cups) dried apricots
1¾ cups rum

juice of 1 lemon
juice of 1 orange
1½ cups granulated sugar

MAKES ABOUT: 1 quart   PREPARATION TIME: 40 minutes, plus 2 weeks maturing and canning (optional)
COOKING TIME: 20 minutes

1 Using a sharp knife, nick or snip the brown outer skins off the chestnuts. Put the chestnuts in a pot, cover with boiling water and boil 3 to 5 minutes. Lift out the chestnuts, a few at a time, and peel off both the outer shell and inner skin.

2 Sterilize a 1-quart canning jar so that it is ready to use (see page 14).

3 Put the prepared chestnuts, apricots, rum and ⅔ cup water in a large heavy pot. Slowly bring to just below boiling point and simmer 10 minutes until the chestnuts are tender.

4 Add the lemon juice, orange juice and sugar to the pot. Stir the ingredients together and bring to a boil, then remove the pot from the heat.

5 Using a slotted spoon, remove the chestnuts and apricots from the pot and pack into the warmed, sterilized jar. Pour in the remaining liquid, covering the chestnuts and apricots completely. Leave a ½-inch gap between the top of the liquid and the lid. Tap the jar lightly on the counter to remove any air bubbles. Fit the sterilized rubber band or metal lid and seal the jar. If using a screw-band jar, loosen by a quarter-turn after sealing. Label and let cool completely before storing in the refrigerator.

6 Let mature 2 weeks before eating and use within 1 month.

7 If you wish to store the preserve for longer, follow the instructions for canning on page 23.

Pears in Mulled Wine

Christmas is the time to serve these pears, when the smell of mulled wine is in the air. Serve as a dessert, and if you have any left over, they are delicious served sliced with cold turkey.

2 pounds, 4 ounces firm pears, peeled, cored and quartered
1⅓ cups red wine
2½ cups granulated sugar

grated zest and juice of 1 lemon
1 Bay Tree mulled wine spice bundle
1 star anise

MAKES ABOUT: 1 quart   PREPARATION TIME: 25 minutes, plus canning (optional)
COOKING TIME: 20 minutes

1 Put the pears in a pot, cover with boiling water and simmer gently about 5 minutes until almost tender. Drain well.

2 Sterilize a 1-quart canning jar so that it is ready to use (see page 14).

3 Put the wine, sugar, lemon zest and juice, mulled wine spice bundle, star anise and 1 cup water in a heavy pot. Bring to a boil, stirring until the sugar has dissolved, and simmer gently 5 minutes.

4 Add the pears to the pot and continue to simmer gently about 5 minutes until the pears are just tender. Test if the pears are cooked by piercing with a knife. If it goes in easily, they are ready.

5 Using a slotted spoon, remove the pears from the pot and pack into the warmed, sterilized jar. Remove the mulled wine spice bundle but leave the star anise.

6 Pour the remaining liquid, including the star anise, over the pears, covering them completely. Leave a ½-inch gap between the top of the liquid and the lid. Tap the jar lightly on the counter to remove any air bubbles. Fit the sterilized rubber band or metal lid and seal the jar. If using a screw-band jar, loosen by a quarter-turn after sealing. Label and let cool completely before storing in the refrigerator. Eat within 1 month.

7 If you wish to store the preserve for longer, follow the instructions for canning on page 23.

Emma's tip Mulled wine has been served as a warming winter drink, especially at Christmas and Halloween, for centuries. Originally, spicing wine improved the flavor of good, though poorly stored wines and was not considered a high-class drink. With this in mind, don't choose a delicate-flavored wine or the cheapest table wine. A fruity, full-bodied red wine that isn't too expensive, such as a cabernet sauvignon, merlot or Syrah, would be ideal.

Spiced Sherry Plums

These lightly spiced plums are best served as a dessert with a little of the sherry syrup poured over them. Add a good spoonful of thick cream or crème fraîche and serve with small, crisp cookies.

½ cup granulated sugar
1 pound, 12 ounces plums
pared zest of 1 orange
1 cinnamon stick

2 star anise
4 whole cloves
generous 1 cup medium-dry sherry

MAKES ABOUT: 1 quart PREPARATION TIME: 55 minutes, plus 30 minutes cooling, 2 weeks maturing and canning (optional) COOKING TIME: 10 minutes

1 Put the sugar and 1 cup water in a large, heavy pot and heat gently, stirring until the sugar has dissolved. Bring to a boil and boil 1 minute. Remove from the heat and stir in a scant 1 cup water.

2 If you like, cut the plums in half and pit them, or leave whole. Add the plums (skin-side down if cut in half), orange zest, cinnamon stick, star anise and cloves to the pot and simmer gently 4 to 5 minutes until the plum skins split. If using whole plums, turn once or twice in the liquid.

3 Drain the plums and spices, reserving the syrup. Let the syrup cool.

4 Using a sharp knife, gently peel the skins from the plums. Discard the skins and let the plums cool.

5 Sterilize a 1-quart canning jar so that it is ready to use (see page 14).

6 Pack the cooled plums and spices into the warmed, sterilized jar. If you have reserved the plum pits, add a few to impart their almond flavor.

7 Add the sherry to the cooled syrup, stir, and then pour the syrup over the plums, covering them completely. Leave a ½-inch gap between the top of the liquid and the lid. Tap the jar lightly on the counter to remove any air bubbles. Fit the sterilized rubber band or metal lid and seal the jar. If using a screw-band jar, loosen by a quarter-turn after sealing. Label and store in the refrigerator.

8 Let mature 2 weeks before eating and use within 1 month.

9 If you wish to store the preserve for longer, follow the instructions for canning on page 23.

Dark Chocolate Sauce

Rich and thick, this is for real chocolate lovers. It can't be kept for a long time but it is unlikely that you will need to! Serve it hot or cold, drizzled over vanilla ice cream, chocolate brownies, strawberries, profiteroles or chocolate cake, or sneak a spoonful from the jar.

½ cup unsalted butter, cut into pieces
1 pound dark chocolate (minimum 70% cocoa
   solids), broken into pieces

1 cup heavy cream

MAKES ABOUT: 1¼ cups PREPARATION TIME: 5 minutes COOKING TIME: 10 minutes

1 Sterilize enough wide-necked jars in the oven so that they are ready to use (see page 14).

2 Put the butter and chocolate in the top of a double boiler set over gently simmering water. Heat gently, stirring the mixture until the butter and chocolate have melted and the mixture has combined.

3 Gradually stir in the cream until the sauce is smooth.

4 The sauce can be used immediately and served hot. To store, pour into the warmed, sterilized jars, seal immediately and label. Let cool completely before storing in the refrigerator up to 3 weeks.

5 Serve cold or, to serve hot, reheat the sauce gently in a pot.

Emma's tip Dark Chocolate Sauce and Butterscotch Sauce freeze well, if you make more than you need. Pour into a plastic container, let cool and then seal and store in the freezer. Let thaw at room temperature about 8 hours before serving. Keep in the refrigerator once opened.

Butterscotch Sauce

Serve this luxurious, traditional sauce poured over ice cream, plum puddings, gingerbread, crêpes and any other of your favorite desserts. Butterscotch sauce doesn't have a long shelf life but if you have any left over you can freeze it and keep to serve with ice cream for a quick dessert.

½ cup plus 1 tablespoon unsalted butter, cut into pieces
scant ⅔ cup light brown sugar

⅓ cup golden syrup (or light corn syrup)
½ teaspoon vanilla extract

MAKES ABOUT: 1¼ cups PREPARATION TIME: 5 minutes COOKING TIME: 10 minutes

1 Sterilize enough wide-necked jars in the oven so that they are ready to use (see page 14).

2 Put the butter, sugar, golden syrup and vanilla extract in the top of a double boiler set over gently simmering water. Heat gently, stirring until the butter has melted, the sugar dissolved, the ingredients are combined and the sauce is smooth.

3 The sauce can be used immediately and served hot. To store, pour into the warmed, sterilized jars, seal immediately and label. Let cool completely before storing in the refrigerator up to 3 weeks.

4 Serve cold or, to serve hot, reheat the sauce gently in a pot.

Elderflower Syrup

Early summer is the time to make this syrup, when you will see elder shrubs and trees covered in pretty white flowers. Collect the flowers when just in bloom and use while very fresh so they retain their fragrant perfume. Elderflower Syrup is delicious with sparkling water and Prosecco, and can also be added to fruit salads, fools and crumbles. It particularly complements gooseberries.

6 ounces elderflower heads (about 25 large heads)   4½ cups granulated sugar
pared zest and juice of 2 lemons

MAKES ABOUT: 6½ cups   PREPARATION TIME: 20 minutes, plus 24 hours infusing
COOKING TIME: 5 minutes

1 Remove any insects from the elderflower heads (there is no need to wash the flowers). Put the elderflowers and lemon zest in a bowl and add 6 cups water. Cover and let infuse in a cool place 24 hours, stirring occasionally as you pass by.

2 The next day, strain the liquid into a preserving pan.

3 Add the lemon juice and sugar to the pan and heat gently, stirring until the sugar has dissolved, then simmer 2 to 3 minutes.

4 Strain the liquid through some cheesecloth.

5 To store, pour the syrup into clean plastic bottles, leaving a 1-inch space at the top to allow for expansion. Label and freeze (see below) until fully frozen.

6 Thaw the syrup at room temperature for about 8 hours. To serve as a drink, dilute to taste with spring water or sparking water. Keep in the refrigerator once they've been opened.

Emma's tip This elderflower syrup recipe uses freezing to stop the fermentation process. This removes the need to use citric acid, which you may find suggested in other recipes. Freeze in plastic bottles to allow for expansion, but you could transfer to glass bottles when thawed if you prefer.

Old-fashioned Lemonade

This traditional sweet and sour drink is popular with adults and children; perhaps it is nostalgia and the thought of long summers spent lazily in the sunshine as a child. It is certainly far superior to any commercial product you can buy. Tastes have changed over the years, and archive recipes use fewer lemons and more sugar. You can adjust the taste to your liking by adding more lemon juice or sugar before storing.

6 lemons
¾ cup granulated sugar

lemon slices and mint sprigs, to serve

MAKES ABOUT: 6½ cups   PREPARATION TIME: 20 minutes, plus 12 hours (or overnight infusing)
COOKING TIME: 10 minutes

1 Using a potato peeler, thinly pare the zest from the lemons. Do not include any pith or it will make the lemonade taste bitter.

2 Put the lemon zest, sugar and 6 cups water in a large pot and slowly bring to a boil, stirring to dissolve the sugar. Reduce the heat and simmer 5 minutes.

3 Pour the syrup into a large bowl, heatproof measuring cup or pitcher, cover and let infuse 12 hours or overnight in a cool place.

4 The next day, squeeze the juice from the lemons. Strain the cooled syrup through a strainer into a clean large bowl or pitcher. Add the lemon juice and stir together.

5 To store, pour the lemonade into clean plastic bottles, leaving 1 inch to allow for expansion. Label and freeze (see page 115) until fully frozen.

6 Thaw at room temperature about 8 hours and then serve chilled with lemon slices and mint sprigs. Keep in the refrigerator once opened and use within 2 days.

Crème de Cassis

This black currant liqueur is what you use to make the French apéritif kir. Pour a splash of crème de cassis into a glass and top up with white wine. There is also Kir Royale, made with champagne; Kir Pétillant, made with sparkling wine; Kir Normand, made with Normandy cider; and Kir Breton, made with Breton cider. Two other liqueurs that can be made in the same way are framboise, with raspberries, and crème de mûre, with blackberries.

2 pounds (about 10 cups) black currants, stripped
4 cups brandy, gin or vodka

¾ cup granulated sugar per cups of liquid

MAKES ABOUT: 6½ cups   PREPARATION TIME: 35 minutes, plus 8 weeks macerating, and 48 hours and 6 months maturing

1 Sterilize a large enough jar that will hold the black currants and liquor (see page 14).

2 Put the black currants in a bowl and crush with a fork. Put them in the sterilized jar and pour in the liquor. Cover with a tight-fitting lid and leave the jar in a cool, dark place for 8 weeks.

3 After the black currants have macerated, strain the mixture through a strainer into a large measuring cup or pitcher.

4 Measure the liquid and for each 2 cups of liquid, add ¾ cup sugar.

5 Pour the mixture into a large pitcher or bowl, cover and leave at room temperature 48 hours, stirring occasionally as you pass by to dissolve the sugar.

6 Sterilize enough bottles so that they are ready to use (see page 14).

7 Line a strainer with cheesecloth and strain the mixture. Pour the liqueur into the sterilized bottles, seal and label.

8 Store the liqueur in a cool, dry, dark place for 6 months before using.

Emma's tip To strip black currants easily from their stalks, hold each stalk at the top of the bunch over a bowl and run a fork firmly down the stem. The black currants should then come away easily.

Limoncello

This is a wonderful homemade version of the sweet, lemony Italian liqueur. Serve it as they do in Italy, either before a meal or afterwards, in small glasses, poured over ice cubes. Otherwise, drizzle over vanilla ice cream or strawberries.

6 lemons
4¼ cups vodka

2½ cups granulated sugar

MAKES ABOUT: 1½ quarts PREPARATION TIME: 35 minutes, plus 2 to 3 hours cooling, 10 days macerating and 10 days infusing COOKING TIME: 5 minutes

1 Sterilize a 1½- or 2-quart jar so that it is ready to use (see page 14).

2 Using a potato peeler, thinly pare the zest from the lemons. Do not include any pith or it will make the limoncello taste bitter.

3 Put the lemon zest in the warmed, sterilized jar and pour in the vodka. Cover with a tight-fitting lid and leave the jar in a light place at room temperature for at least 10 days. Turn the jar once a day to agitate the zest.

4 After the lemon zest has macerated, put the sugar and 2 cups water in a large pot and slowly bring to a boil, stirring to dissolve the sugar. Reduce the heat and simmer 5 minutes. Remove from the heat and let it sit 2 to 3 hours until completely cold.

5 Add the lemon zest and vodka mixture to the cooled syrup and stir together.

6 Sterilize 1 large or several small jars. Pour the mixture into the jars and let it infuse for 10 more days for the flavors to develop. This time there is no need to shake the jar (or jars).

7 Sterilize enough freezerproof plastic or glass bottles so that they are ready to use (see page 14).

8 Line a strainer with cheesecloth and strain the mixture. Pour the limoncello into the sterilized bottles. Seal and label. Store the bottles in the freezer.

Emma's tip It is safe to store glass bottles of limoncello in the freezer, as vodka does not freeze in domestic freezers, so will not expand.

Sloe Gin

Sloes are wild plums which can be found in hedgerows in the fall but the best time to collect them is when the first frosts have arrived. The frost breaks down the sloes, which helps to release their juices and flavor. You can gather sloes earlier and put them in the freezer to get the same effect; this may mean you get to the sloes before the birds do, too!

1 pound, 2 ounces (3¼ cups) sloes
1¾ cups granulated sugar

3¼ cups gin

MAKES ABOUT: 1 quart PREPARATION TIME: 45 minutes, plus 11 weeks macerating and 12 months maturing (optional)

1 Sterilize enough jars for the sloes to half-fill them, and have the jars ready to use (see page 14).

2 If the sloes haven't been affected by the frost or you have not frozen them, prick each sloe several times with a sewing needle.

3 Half-fill the warmed, sterilized jars with the sloes. Divide the sugar equally among the jars and pour the gin over the sloes. Cover with tight-fitting lids and shake the jars well.

4 Set the jars in a cool, dry, dark place. Shake once a day for 1 week, and then once a week for 10 weeks.

5 Sterilize enough bottles so that they are ready to use (see page 14).

6 Line a strainer with cheesecloth and strain the mixture. Pour the liqueur into the sterilized bottles, seal and label. Store in a cool, dry, dark place. The liqueur can be drunk immediately but ideally should be stored 1 year before drinking.

Chutneys &
Relishes

Pear & Ginger Chutney

A sweet and spicy chutney and, if you like ginger, you will find it difficult to resist another spoonful! It gets even better as it matures and is particularly good served with pork, as an accompaniment to curry or with cold meats, cheese and bread.

2½ cups red wine vinegar
4 pounds, 8 ounces pears, peeled, cored and chopped
¾ ounce (about 3 tablespoons) ginger root, peeled and finely chopped
2½ ounces (scant ½ cup) preserved ginger, finely chopped

12 ounces (about 2½ cups) onions, chopped
2½ cups granulated sugar
grated zest and juice of 2 oranges
½ teaspoon ground cloves

MAKES ABOUT: 3 pounds, 5 ounces (5 cups) PREPARATION TIME: 35 minutes, plus 1 month maturing COOKING TIME: 2 hours 5 minutes

1 Pour the vinegar into a preserving pan. Add all the remaining ingredients, stir together and slowly bring to a boil.

2 Reduce the heat and simmer about 2 hours or until no excess liquid remains and the mixture is thick. Stir from time to time to prevent the mixture from sticking to the bottom of the pan.

3 Meanwhile, sterilize enough jars with non-metallic, vinegar-proof lids, or canning jars, so that they are ready to use (see page 14).

4 Spoon the chutney into the warmed, sterilized jars. Seal immediately, label and store in a cool, dry, dark place.

5 Let them mature at least 1 month before using. Refrigerate after opening.

Flaming Mango Chutney

This spicy, fresh-tasting Indian chutney is the perfect addition to any curry, particularly a lamb or chicken-based recipe. It is also delicious simply scooped up with poppadums, parathas or chapatis.

1¼ cups white wine vinegar
⅓ red Thai chili, finely chopped, seeds reserved
4 garlic cloves, finely chopped
2½ cups Demerara sugar

2 tablespoons garlic paste
3 tablespoons ground cumin
2½ teaspoons salt
2 mangoes, pitted, peeled and roughly chopped

MAKES ABOUT: 3 pounds (4½ to 5 cups) PREPARATION TIME: 35 minutes, plus 1 month maturing
COOKING TIME: 1¼ hours

1 Pour the vinegar into a preserving pan. Add all the remaining ingredients, except the mangoes, and slowly bring to a boil. Add the chili seeds if you like a hot flavor.

2 Reduce the heat and boil gently about 10 minutes, stirring occasionally, until the mixture is reduced by a third.

3 Add the mangoes to the pan and simmer gently 1 hour until the mango has softened but still holds its shape and there is no excess liquid in the pan. Stir from time to time to prevent the mixture from sticking to the bottom of the pan.

4 Meanwhile, sterilize enough jars with non-metallic, vinegar-proof lids, or canning jars, so that they are ready to use (see page 14).

5 Spoon the chutney into the warmed, sterilized jars. Seal immediately, label and store in a cool, dry, dark place.

6 Let them mature at least 1 month before using. Refrigerate after opening.

Gingered Plum Chutney

Flavored with ginger and allspice (a spice in its own right that tastes like cloves, nutmeg and cinnamon) this chutney is perfect to serve with crusty bread and cheese. Dry, sharp cheeses, such as feta and goat cheese, work particularly well as they contrast with the sweetness of the chutney.

1 cup red wine vinegar
2 pounds, 4 ounces plums, cut in half, pitted and chopped
1 pound, 2 ounces (about 5 cups) cooking apples, peeled, cored and chopped

1¾ cups light brown sugar
1 heaped tablespoon ginger paste
1 tablespoon ground allspice

MAKES ABOUT: 2 pounds (3 to 3½ cups) PREPARATION TIME: 30 minutes, plus 1 month maturing
COOKING TIME: 1 hour 20 minutes

1 Pour the vinegar into a preserving pan. Add all the remaining ingredients, stir together and slowly bring to a boil.

2 Reduce the heat and simmer gently about 1¼ hours until the mixture is light brown and thick. Stir occasionally to prevent the mixture from sticking to the bottom of the pan.

3 Meanwhile, sterilize enough jars with non-metallic, vinegar-proof lids, or canning jars, so that they are ready to use (see page 14).

4 Spoon the chutney into the warmed, sterilized jars. Seal immediately, label and store in a cool, dry, dark place.

5 Let them mature at least 1 month before using. Refrigerate after opening.

Spicy Rhubarb & Orange Chutney

There is more to do with rhubarb than putting it in a crumble! This mildly spiced chutney complements smoked mackerel, cold ham or hot smoked ham steaks. It is also delicious served with a cheeseboard.

1¾ cups red wine vinegar

2 cups light brown sugar

2 pounds, 4 ounces (8 to 9 cups) pink rhubarb, chopped

2 pounds, 4 ounces red onions, finely chopped

6 garlic cloves, finely chopped

7 ounces (about 1 cup) tomatoes, chopped

grated zest and juice of 4 oranges

2 teaspoons ground ginger

1 teaspoon ground cinnamon

¼ teaspoon ground cloves

MAKES ABOUT: 3 pounds (4½ to 5 cups) PREPARATION TIME: 35 minutes, plus 1 month maturing
COOKING TIME: 1 hour 35 minutes

1 Put the vinegar, sugar and ½ cup water in a preserving pan and slowly bring to a boil, stirring until the sugar has dissolved.

2 Add the rhubarb, onions, garlic, tomatoes, orange juice, ginger, cinnamon and cloves to the pan. Reduce the heat and simmer gently about 1½ hours or until no excess liquid remains and the mixture is thick. Stir from time to time to prevent the mixture from sticking to the bottom of the pan.

3 Meanwhile, sterilize enough jars with non-metallic, vinegar-proof lids, or canning jars, so that they are ready to use (see page 14).

4 Add the orange zest to the pan and stir together.

5 Spoon the chutney into the warmed, sterilized jars. Seal immediately, label and store in a cool, dry, dark place.

6 Let them mature at least 1 month before using. Refrigerate after opening.

Indian Lime Chutney

Often referred to as a pickle but actually a chutney, this tangy preserve goes well with Indian curries but also with Middle Eastern foods such as lamb and couscous.

6 limes
heaped ⅓ cup coarse salt
¼ cup canola oil
2 teaspoons mustard seeds
4 garlic cloves, finely chopped
2 teaspoons ginger paste
½ teaspoon chili powder

1 teaspoon mustard powder
2 teaspoons ground fenugreek
2 teaspoons paprika
1 teaspoon turmeric
1¼ cups distilled white vinegar
1¼ cups Demerara sugar

MAKES ABOUT: 1 pound, 12 ounces (2½ to 3 cups) PREPARATION TIME: 30 minutes, plus 48 hours curing and 1 month maturing COOKING TIME: 1½ to 2 hours

1 Cut the limes into eighths and then cut each eighth into 4 pieces. Discard the seeds. Put the lime pieces in a large bowl and sprinkle the salt over them. Cover the bowl and let it cure in a cool place 48 hours, stirring occasionally.

2 Drain the limes, rinse well under cold running water and drain.

3 Heat the oil in a large, heavy pot. Add the mustard seeds and cook 30 seconds, or until they start to jump in the pan (be careful as they can burn you). Add the garlic, ginger paste, chili powder, mustard powder, fenugreek, paprika and turmeric and cook 30 seconds to allow the spices to release their flavor.

4 Add the vinegar and lime pieces to the pot, return to a boil, then reduce the heat and simmer gently 1 hour. Stir occasionally to prevent the mixture from sticking to the bottom of the pot.

5 Add the sugar to the pot and slowly bring to a boil, stirring until the sugar has dissolved. Reduce the heat and simmer gently 5 minutes, stirring all the time. Be very careful toward the end of cooking that it does not become too thick, as it thickens even more as it cools.

6 Meanwhile, sterilize enough jars with non-metallic, vinegar-proof lids, or canning jars, so that they are ready to use (see page 14).

7 Spoon the chutney into the warmed, sterilized jars. Seal immediately, label and store in a cool, dry, dark place.

8 Let them mature at least 1 month before using. Refrigerate after opening.

Curried Apricot & Apple Chutney

This chutney has several uses and it goes particularly well with chicken. Serve a spoonful as an accompaniment to cold chicken, or add a spoonful to yogurt and use as a dressing for a chicken salad, or to mayonnaise to make the British sandwich filling Coronation Chicken. Alternatively, add to a stuffing mix to serve with roast chicken.

1 cup coconut milk
1½ teaspoons curry powder
¾ teaspoon ginger paste
¾ cup cider vinegar
6 ounces (about 1½ cups) onions, chopped

1 pound, 2 ounces (2¾ cups) dried apricots, chopped
15 ounces (4 to 4½ cups) cooking apples, peeled, cored and chopped
¾ cup granulated sugar

MAKES ABOUT: 2 pounds, 12 ounces (4 to 4½ cups) PREPARATION TIME: 35 minutes, plus 1 month maturing
COOKING TIME: 50 minutes

1 Put the coconut milk in a large measuring cup, add the curry powder and ginger paste and mix together.

2 Pour the curried coconut milk and vinegar into a preserving pan. Add the onions, apricots, apples and sugar, stir together and slowly bring to a boil.

3 Reduce the heat and simmer gently about 45 minutes until the onions and apricots are soft and no excess liquid remains. Do not let the mixture get too thick. Stir regularly to prevent the mixture from sticking to the bottom of the pan.

4 Meanwhile, sterilize enough jars with non-metallic, vinegar-proof lids, or canning jars, so that they are ready to use (see page 14).

5 Spoon the chutney into the warmed, sterilized jars. Seal immediately, label and store in a cool, dry, dark place.

6 Let them mature at least 1 month before using. Refrigerate after opening.

Emma's tip Use yellow dried apricots if you can find them, rather than already plumped or brown dried apricots, as the color is much better for this preserve.

Apricot & Walnut Chutney

This uncomplicated recipe makes a light, fresh chutney with the additional crunch of chopped walnuts. It is the perfect addition to a cheeseboard or a lamb, pork or poultry dish whether the meat is served hot or cold.

1¾ cups cider vinegar

2 pounds, 4 ounces apricots, pitted and chopped

1 pound, 2 ounces (about 4 to 4½ cups) red onions, finely chopped

1½ ounces (⅓ cup) ginger root, peeled and finely chopped

7 ounces (scant 1½ cups) golden raisins

2½ cups Demerara sugar

grated zest and juice of 1 orange

½ teaspoon ground cinnamon

1 teaspoon salt

1½ cups walnuts, chopped

MAKES ABOUT: 3 pounds, 12 ounces (5½ to 6 cups)   PREPARATION TIME: 30 minutes, plus 1 month maturing
COOKING TIME: 1½ hours

1 Pour the vinegar and 1 cup water into a preserving pan. Add all the remaining ingredients, stir together and slowly bring to a boil.

2 Reduce the heat and simmer about 1½ hours until no excess liquid remains and the mixture is thick. Stir from time to time to prevent the mixture from sticking to the bottom of the pan.

3 Meanwhile, sterilize enough jars with non-metallic, vinegar-proof lids, or canning jars, so that they are ready to use (see page 14).

4 Spoon the chutney into the warmed, sterilized jars. Seal immediately, label and store in a cool, dry, dark place.

5 Let them mature at least 1 month before using. Refrigerate after opening.

Emma's tip You can make variations of this recipe by replacing the apricots with peaches or nectarines and the walnuts with pecans. You can also use dried apricots as opposed to fresh and, if you choose these, you will need 1 pound, 9 ounces, which should be soaked in water for 12 hours and then drained (or use already plumped dried apricots, and skip the soaking).

Banana & Date Chutney

Like most chutneys, this is an excellent accompaniment to curries, particularly spicy chicken recipes. It also goes well with cold turkey and chicken, as the sweetness of the fruits enhances the taste of the poultry.

½ teaspoon cumin seeds
2 cups cider vinegar
2 pounds, 12 ounces bananas, peeled and sliced
9 ounces fresh or dried dates, cut in half and pitted
9 ounces (about 2 cups) onions, chopped
1½ cups granulated sugar

1 teaspoon ginger paste
½ teaspoon chili powder
1½ teaspoons ground mace
½ teaspoon salt
grated zest and juice of 1 orange

MAKES ABOUT: 3 pounds, 12 ounces (5½ to 6 cups)   PREPARATION TIME: 35 minutes, plus 1 month maturing
COOKING TIME: 40 minutes

1 Put the cumin seeds in a nonstick skillet and dry-fry, tossing continuously, about 1 minute until golden brown.

2 Pour the vinegar and 2 cups water into a preserving pan. Add all the remaining ingredients, except the orange zest and juice, stir together and slowly bring to a boil.

3 Reduce the heat and simmer gently about 30 minutes until the onions are soft and only a little liquid remains on the surface. Do not let the mixture get too thick and dark. Stir regularly to mix the ingredients and prevent the mixture from sticking to the bottom of the pan.

4 Meanwhile, sterilize enough jars with non-metallic, vinegar-proof lids, or canning jars, so that they are ready to use (see page 14).

5 Stir the orange zest and juice into the cooked chutney and simmer 5 minutes more.

6 Spoon the chutney into the warmed, sterilized jars. Seal immediately, label and store in a cool, dry, dark place.

7 Let them mature at least 1 month before using. Refrigerate after opening.

Green Tomato Chutney

An old favorite, just like your grandmother used to make. If you have any unripened tomatoes at the end of the season, this is the classic recipe to use them up. Use Green Tomato Chutney to enhance any dish, and it is delicious in sandwiches, of course.

2 teaspoons pickling spices
1¾ cups distilled white vinegar
1 pound, 2 ounces green tomatoes, chopped
1 pound, 2 ounces (4 to 4½ cups) cooking apples, peeled, cored and chopped
14 ounces (about 3 cups) onions, chopped
7 ounces (scant 1½ cups) raisins

2 cups Demerara sugar
1 garlic clove, chopped
½ teaspoon cayenne pepper
1 teaspoon ground ginger
1 teaspoon salt

MAKES ABOUT: 2 pounds, 12 ounces (4 to 4½ cups) PREPARATION TIME: 40 minutes, plus 1 month maturing COOKING TIME: 1 hour 35 minutes

1 Tie the pickling spices in some cheesecloth.

2 Pour the vinegar into a preserving pan. Add the cheesecloth bag and all the remaining ingredients, stir together and slowly bring to a boil.

3 Reduce the heat and simmer about 1½ hours or until the mixture is dark and thick and only a little liquid remains on the surface. Do not let the mixture get too thick. Stir regularly to prevent the mixture from sticking to the bottom of the pan.

4 Meanwhile, sterilize enough jars with non-metallic, vinegar-proof lids, or canning jars, so that they are ready to use (see page 14).

5 Spoon the chutney into the warmed, sterilized jars. Seal immediately, label and store in a cool, dry, dark place.

6 Let them mature at least 1 month before using. Refrigerate after opening.

Emma's tip If you would like to make your own pickling spices, combine equal quantities of coriander seeds, yellow mustard seeds and whole allspice in a jar and add a few whole cloves and peppercorns. Use as required, adding a bay leaf and cinnamon stick before cooking. You need 1 ounce for every 4 cups vinegar.

Carrot & Date Chutney

The texture of this chutney is slightly crunchy and apart from serving it with cheese and cold meats, it would make a good addition to a stuffing mix. An alternative suggestion is to spread it inside small pita breads, top with thin slices of chicken or lamb and serve with minted yogurt and a wedge of lime.

1½ tablespoons pickling spices
1¾ cups cider vinegar
10 ounces (about 2½ cups) onions, finely chopped

1 pound, 2 ounces (6 to 7 medium) carrots, grated
15 ounces pitted dried dates, chopped
1¼ cups granulated sugar

MAKES ABOUT: 3 pounds, 5 ounces (5 cups)   PREPARATION TIME: 35 minutes, plus 1 month maturing
COOKING TIME: 1 hour

1 Tie the pickling spices in some cheesecloth.

2 Pour the vinegar and 4 cups water into a preserving pan. Add the cheesecloth bag, onions, carrots, dates and sugar, stir together and slowly bring to a boil.

3 Reduce the heat and simmer about 1 hour or until no excess liquid remains. Do not let the mixture get too thick. Stir regularly to prevent the mixture from sticking to the bottom of the pan.

4 Meanwhile, sterilize enough jars with non-metallic, vinegar-proof lids, or canning jars, so that they are ready to use (see page 14).

5 Spoon the chutney into the warmed, sterilized jars. Seal immediately, label and store in a cool, dry, dark place.

6 Let them mature at least 1 month before using. Refrigerate after opening.

Emma's tip The recipe suggests using pitted, dried dates but fresh dates can also be used. Remove the pits first; slit each date open lengthwise and push the pit out with your fingers. Use ½ cup less water during cooking.

Indian Tomato & Nigella Seed Chutney

Nigella seeds are sometimes referred to as black onion or black cumin seeds, but they are not connected to either and are the seeds of *nigella sativa*, an annual flowering herb. This sweet chutney is a delicious accompaniment to serve with your favorite curry.

4 pounds, 8 ounces tomatoes
2½ cups distilled white vinegar
5 cups granulated sugar
8 garlic cloves, crushed
4 teaspoons nigella seeds
¾ cup raisins

⅓ cup blanched almonds, chopped
1 teaspoon red pepper flakes
3 bay leaves
1 teaspoon salt

MAKES ABOUT: 2 pounds, 2 ounces (3 to 3½ cups) PREPARATION TIME: 40 minutes
COOKING TIME: 1 hour 35 minutes

1 With a sharp knife, cut a cross in the skin of each tomato, then put in a heatproof bowl and cover with boiling water. Let stand for 2 to 3 minutes, then drain. Peel off and discard the skins. Roughly chop the flesh.

2 Put the tomatoes, vinegar and 1¼ cups water in a preserving pan. Add all the remaining ingredients, stir together and slowly bring to a boil.

3 Reduce the heat and simmer about 1½ hours until no excess liquid remains. Stir from time to time to prevent the mixture from sticking to the bottom of the pan. Remove and discard the bay leaves.

4 Meanwhile, sterilize enough jars with non-metallic, vinegar-proof lids, or canning jars, so that they are ready to use (see page 14).

5 Spoon the chutney into the warmed, sterilized jars. Seal immediately and label. The chutney can be eaten immediately and doesn't need to mature. Refrigerate after opening.

Beet & Orange Chutney

This is a chutney for beet lovers. Lightly spiced and a wonderful vivid, ruby red color, it is best served with pork or cheese, particularly goat cheese or a tasty sharp cheddar. If you have a little over when you come to putting it in the jars, save it to serve warm with, for example, roast pork, grilled sausages or hot dogs, or a beef stew.

2 cups red wine vinegar

2 pounds, 4 ounces raw beets, peeled and cubed

1 pound, 10 ounces (about 6½ cups) cooking apples, peeled, cored and chopped

12 ounces (about 2¾ cups) onions, chopped

2½ cups granulated sugar

1 teaspoon grated nutmeg

1 teaspoon pumpkin pie spice

1½ teaspoons ground cloves

grated zest and juice of 1 orange

MAKES ABOUT: 3 pounds, 12 ounces (5½ to 6 cups) PREPARATION TIME: 40 minutes, plus 1 month maturing COOKING TIME: 2½ hours

1 Pour the vinegar into a preserving pan. Add all the remaining ingredients, except the orange zest and juice, stir together and slowly bring to a boil.

2 Reduce the heat and simmer about 2¼ hours until the mixture is thick and only a little liquid remains on the surface. Stir occasionally to prevent the mixture from sticking to the bottom of the pan.

3 Meanwhile, sterilize enough jars with non-metallic, vinegar-proof lids, or canning jars, so that they are ready to use (see page 14).

4 Stir the orange zest and juice into the pan. Increase the heat and cook about 5 minutes until only a little liquid remains on the surface. Do not let the mixture get too dark. Stir regularly to prevent the mixture from sticking to the bottom of the pan.

5 Spoon the chutney into the warmed, sterilized jars. Seal immediately, label and store in a cool, dry, dark place.

6 Let them mature at least 1 month before using. Refrigerate after opening.

Emma's tip Beet juices stain so if you want to avoid bright red hands, wear protective rubber or disposable gloves when preparing it and use a plastic chopping board rather than a wooden one. Alternatively, you could use golden beets; they have a more subtle flavor than red beets but also have a beautiful, vibrant color that doesn't stain.

Cool Chili & Apple Chutney

If you like something with just a little heat (hence its name), this spicy apple chutney is the perfect partner for cheese and cold meats. It also works very well served with roast pork as an alternative to applesauce.

2 cups cider vinegar

2 pounds, 4 ounces (about 10 cups) eating apples, peeled, cored and chopped

10 ounces (about 2½ cups) onions, chopped

2 cups Demerara sugar

7 ounces (about 2 cups) red bell peppers, cut in half lengthwise, seeded and chopped

1 teaspoon red pepper flakes

2 tablespoons peeled and grated ginger root

½ teaspoon grated nutmeg

½ teaspoon ground allspice

¼ teaspoon ground cloves

2 teaspoons salt

MAKES ABOUT: 2 pounds, 4 ounces (3½ cups) PREPARATION TIME: 35 minutes, plus 1 month maturing
COOKING TIME: 1 hour 35 minutes

1 Pour the vinegar and 2 cups water into a preserving pan. Add all the remaining ingredients, stir together and slowly bring to a boil.

2 Reduce the heat and simmer 1½ hours or until no excess liquid remains and the mixture is thick. Stir from time to time to prevent the mixture from sticking to the bottom of the pan.

3 Meanwhile, sterilize enough jars with non-metallic, vinegar-proof lids, or canning jars, so that they are ready to use (see page 14).

4 Spoon the chutney into the warmed, sterilized jars. Seal immediately, label and store in a cool, dry, dark place.

5 Let them mature at least 1 month before using. Refrigerate after opening.

Fig & Balsamic Relish

With its sweet and sour flavor, this distinctive relish is best served with cold meats or chicken liver pâté or cheese, particularly a salty sheep or tangy goat cheese. The recipe suggests using dried figs, as they are less expensive and readily available, but you could use 20 to 22 fresh figs instead if you have a bumper harvest.

1 tablespoon olive oil
1 pound, 2 ounces (4 cups) red onions, sliced
9 ounces (2½ cups) cooking apples, peeled, cored and chopped
⅔ cup balsamic vinegar
⅓ cup sherry vinegar
1 teaspoon ginger paste

1 pound, 2 ounces (heaped 3 cups) dried figs, roughly chopped
5½ ounces (heaped ¾ cup) dried apricots, roughly chopped
grated zest and juice of 2 oranges
¾ teaspoon salt

MAKES ABOUT: 4 pounds (6 to 6½ cups) PREPARATION TIME: 40 minutes, plus 1 month maturing
COOKING TIME: 55 minutes

1 Heat the oil in a preserving pan. Add the onions and fry gently about 15 minutes until softened and beginning to turn brown.

2 Add the apples, balsamic vinegar, sherry vinegar, ginger paste and 2 cups water to the pan. Bring to a boil, then reduce the heat and simmer 15 minutes, stirring occasionally, until the onions are soft.

3 Add the figs, apricots, orange juice and salt to the pan and continue to simmer gently about 20 minutes until only a little liquid remains in the bottom of the pan and the mixture is soft and combined but not too thick. Stir occasionally to prevent the mixture from sticking to the bottom of the pan.

4 Meanwhile, sterilize enough jars with non-metallic, vinegar-proof lids, or canning jars, so that they are ready to use (see page 14).

5 Add the orange zest to the pan and stir together.

6 Spoon the relish into the warmed, sterilized jars. Seal immediately, label and store in a cool, dry, dark place.

7 Let them mature at least 1 month before using. Refrigerate after opening.

Emma's tip When chopping dried figs, dip the knife into hot water occasionally as this helps to stop them from sticking to the knife.

Beet & Horseradish Relish

The beets are crunchy and sweet with just a minor kick added by the horseradish. It is a relish that is excellent as a cold accompaniment with smoked fish, cold meats or cheese. You can also warm it to serve with roast beef.

2 cups red wine vinegar

2 pounds, 4 ounces fresh beets, peeled and cut into small cubes

1 pound, 10 ounces (7 to 8 cups) cooking apples, peeled, cored and chopped

3⅔ cups soft light brown sugar

4¾ ounces grated horseradish

MAKES ABOUT: 2 pounds, 12 ounces (4 to 4½ cups) COOKING TIME: 35 minutes

PREPARATION TIME: 30 minutes, plus 1 month maturing

1 Pour the vinegar into a preserving pan. Add all the ingredients except the horseradish, stir together and slowly bring to a boil.

2 Reduce the heat and simmer about 15 minutes until the apples start to soften.

3 Add the horseradish, bring to a boil and boil about 15 minutes until the mixture is thick and no excess liquid remains in the bottom of the pan. Stir from time to time to prevent the mixture from sticking to the bottom of the pan. Do not overcook or the mixture will turn brown.

4 Meanwhile, sterilize enough jars with non-metallic, vinegar-proof lids, or canning jars, so that they are ready to use (see page 14).

5 Spoon the relish into the warmed, sterilized jars. Seal immediately, label and store in a cool, dry, dark place.

6 Let them mature at least 1 month before using. Refrigerate after opening.

Mostarda di Frutta

This Italian relish is made with seasonal fruits flavored with mustard syrup. Quinces and grapes are the most traditional ingredients, but you can use whichever orchard and vine fruits you have. It is usually served with *bollito misto* or cold meats and cheese.

2 pounds, 12 ounces mixed, small fruits, such as apples, pears, quinces, apricots, peaches, plums, figs, cherries and grapes
1 to 2 teaspoons lemon juice if using apples, pears or quinces

scant 2½ cups white wine vinegar
3¾ cups granulated sugar
¼ cup mustard powder

MAKES ABOUT: 4 to 4½ cups PREPARATION TIME: 50 minutes, plus 48 hours marinating and 2 weeks maturing COOKING TIME: 35 minutes

1 Peel, quarter and core any apples, pears or quinces, and toss in lemon juice. If using apricots, peaches and plums, cut in half and remove the pits. Cut any figs in half. Pit the cherries. Leave the grapes whole.

2 Pour the vinegar into a preserving pan and add the sugar. Slowly bring to a boil, stirring until the sugar dissolves. Reduce the heat to a simmer.

3 Add the fruit to the pan in batches, starting with the firmest and largest such as apples and pears, and ending with the softest and smallest such as grapes, as the fruits will cook at different times. Cook each fruit 2 to 10 minutes, turning in the syrup several times, until tender but not soft. If any skins peel off, discard.

4 Using a slotted spoon, transfer the fruit to a large bowl. Pour the syrup over them, cover and leave at room temperature for 24 hours.

5 The next day, using a slotted spoon, transfer the fruits to another large bowl and pour the syrup into a pan. Bring the syrup to a boil, then reduce the heat and simmer 10 minutes. Pour the syrup

over the fruits, cover and leave at room temperature for another 24 hours.

6 On the third day, sterilize enough canning jars so that they are ready to use (see page 14). Repeat transferring the fruit to a bowl and simmering the syrup. Return the fruits to the pan and bring to a boil.

7 Using a slotted spoon, remove the fruits from the pan and put them in the warmed jars. Divide the types of fruit equally into the jars, arranging in layers.

8 Blend the mustard powder with 3 tablespoons water. Stir it into the syrup and bring slowly to a boil.

9 Pour the syrup into the jars, covering the fruits. Leave a ½-inch gap between the top of the liquid and the lid. Fit the sterilized rubber band or metal lid and seal the jars. If using a screw-band jar, loosen by a quarter-turn after sealing.

10 Label and store in a cool, dry, dark place. Leave to mature at least 2 weeks before using. Refrigerate after opening and use within 1 month.

Sweet & Sour Cucumber Relish

It was in 1994 that an encounter over a jar of homemade cucumber relish, served with cheese, led to the founding of The Bay Tree. We still sell a version of the original and it is very good served with cheese, smoked fish and cold meats due to its refreshing flavor and crisp texture.

2 pounds, 4 ounces (about 3 large) English cucumbers, thinly sliced
2 onions, thinly sliced
⅓ cup coarse salt
2 cups white wine vinegar

scant 2 cups granulated sugar
1 tablespoon mustard seeds
4 whole cloves
½ teaspoon turmeric

MAKES ABOUT: 2 pounds, 4 ounces (3½ cups) PREPARATION TIME: 30 minutes, plus 48 hours salting and 1 month maturing COOKING TIME: 15 minutes

1 Put the cucumber and onion slices in a large bowl and sprinkle the salt over them. Cover the bowl and leave in it a cool place 48 hours, stirring occasionally.

2 Drain the cucumbers and onions, rinse well under cold running water and drain.

3 Sterilize enough jars with non-metallic, vinegar-proof lids, or two x 1-pint canning jars, so that they are ready to use (see page 14).

4 Pour the vinegar into a preserving pan. Add the sugar, mustard seeds, cloves and turmeric and slowly bring to a boil, stirring until the sugar has dissolved completely.

5 Add the cucumbers and onions to the pan, return to a boil and boil 1 minute. Remove the pan from the heat.

6 Using a slotted spoon, pack the cucumber and onions into the warmed, sterilized jars. Return the pan to the heat, bring the liquid to a boil and simmer 5 to 10 minutes until reduced slightly. Be careful that the syrup does not caramelize.

7 Pour the syrup over the cucumbers and onions to cover. Seal immediately, label and store in a cool, dry, dark place.

8 Let them mature at least 1 month before using. Refrigerate after opening.

Butternut Squash Relish with Toasted Seeds

A relish packed with Middle Eastern flavors with a pleasing crunch from the toasted butternut squash seeds. Serve with salads, tagines, kebabs and any chicken or lamb recipes that contain similar spicing.

2 pounds, 4 ounces (about 1) butternut squash
1 teaspoon olive oil
2½ cups white wine vinegar
7 ounces (about 2 cups) cooking apples, peeled, cored and diced
7 ounces (about 1¾ cups) onions, chopped
¾ cup raisins

grated zest and juice of 1 orange
1 cup granulated sugar
1 teaspoon ground ginger
1½ teaspoons ground cinnamon
1½ teaspoons ground cumin
½ teaspoon salt

MAKES ABOUT: 3 pounds, 5 ounces (5 cups)   PREPARATION TIME: 40 minutes, plus 1 month maturing
COOKING TIME: 50 minutes

1 Peel the squash, cut in half and, using a spoon, scoop out the seeds and pulp. Discard the pulp but reserve the seeds. Peel and chop the squash into ½-inch cubes.

2 Heat the oil in a skillet. Add the reserved seeds and cook 30 seconds or until they start to jump in the pan (be careful as they can burn you). Remove from the pan and let cool.

3 Meanwhile, put all the ingredients, except the squash and seeds, in a preserving pan. Add 2½ cups water, stir together and slowly bring to a boil. Reduce the heat and simmer about 10 minutes until the apples start to soften.

4 Add the squash, return to a boil, then reduce the heat and simmer about 30 minutes until the squash

is soft, but still retains its shape. The mixture should be thick with no excess liquid remaining in the bottom of the pan. Stir from time to time to prevent the mixture from sticking to the bottom of the pan.

5 Meanwhile, sterilize enough jars with non-metallic, vinegar-proof lids, or canning jars, so that they are ready to use (see page 14).

6 Add the toasted seeds to the pan and stir together.

7 Spoon the relish into the warmed, sterilized jars. Seal immediately, label and store in a cool, dry, dark place.

8 Let them mature at least 1 month before using. Refrigerate after opening.

Onion Marmalade

Is it a marmalade, a relish or a spread? It doesn't really matter because this sweet and tangy caramelized onion preserve is very versatile. Not only can it be served cold or warm but it is great with almost everything!

1 teaspoon caraway seeds
¾ cup balsamic vinegar
2 pounds, 4 ounces (8 cups) onions, sliced

¼ teaspoon ground cloves
½ teaspoon salt
1¼ cups light brown sugar

MAKES ABOUT: 1 pound, 7 ounces (2 to 2½ cups) PREPARATION TIME: 25 minutes, plus 12 hours or overnight standing and 1 month maturing COOKING TIME: 2¾ hours

1 Put the caraway seeds in a nonstick skillet and dry-fry about 1 minute, tossing continuously, until lightly browned.

2 Put the vinegar, toasted caraway seeds, onions, cloves and salt in a large, heavy pot and slowly bring to a boil. Reduce the heat and simmer gently about 2 hours, stirring occasionally, until the onions are soft and browned and no excess liquid remains in the bottom of the pot.

3 Remove the pot from the heat, cover with a lid and let stand 12 hours or overnight.

4 The next day, add the sugar and bring the mixture to a boil, stirring until the sugar has dissolved. Reduce

the heat and simmer gently, uncovered, about 40 minutes until the mixture is thick. Stir from time to time to prevent the mixture from sticking to the bottom of the pot.

5 Meanwhile, sterilize enough jars with non-metallic, vinegar-proof lids, or canning jars, so that they are ready to use (see page 14).

6 Spoon the marmalade into the warmed, sterilized jars. Seal immediately, label and store in a cool, dry, dark place.

7 Let them mature at least 1 month before using. Refrigerate after opening.

Emma's tip Onion Marmalade has many uses to complement savory foods. A few suggestions include: using it in sandwiches; serving it alongside cheeses, pâtés and cold meats; putting it on sausages, hot dogs, burgers or steaks; adding it to baked potatoes; spreading it on a pizza or in a grilled cheese sandwich; or using a spoonful or two in gravy or mashed potato.

Eggplant & Pepper Relish

A relish for those who love eggplant. It is so delicious you may want to eat chunks right from the jar! It is good served with antipasti, cheeses or curry. Add chopped fresh chili with the garlic if you like extra heat.

1 eggplant, cut into chunks

2 red bell peppers, cut in half lengthwise, seeded and roughly chopped

1 green bell pepper, cut in half lengthwise, seeded and roughly chopped

14 ounces (3½ cups) onions, finely chopped

2 garlic cloves, crushed

1 cup plus 1 tablespoon light brown sugar

¾ cup white wine vinegar

1 teaspoon ground coriander

1 teaspoon paprika

½ teaspoon salt

MAKES ABOUT: 2 pounds, 2 ounces (3 to 3½ cups) PREPARATION TIME: 30 minutes, plus 1 month maturing
COOKING TIME: 1 hour 20 minutes

1 Put the eggplant, bell peppers, onions and garlic in a large, heavy pot. Add ⅓ cup water and slowly bring to a boil.

2 Reduce the heat, cover the pot and simmer gently about 45 minutes, stirring occasionally, until the vegetables are soft.

3 Add the sugar, vinegar, ground coriander, paprika and salt to the pot. Bring to a boil, stirring until the sugar has dissolved.

4 Reduce the heat and simmer about 30 minutes until the mixture is thick yet still chunky. Stir occasionally to prevent the mixture from sticking to the bottom of the pot.

5 Meanwhile, sterilize enough jars with non-metallic, vinegar-proof lids, or canning jars, so that they are ready to use (see page 14).

6 Spoon the relish into the warmed, sterilized jars. Seal immediately, label and store in a cool, dry, dark place.

7 Let them mature at least 1 month before using. Refrigerate after opening.

Caramelized Bell Peppers

A divine sweet and sour combination of peppers with a touch of chili. Serve with cheese, fish, charcuterie, as a pizza topping, a topping for bruschetta or on a baked potato. The bell peppers are wonderful served either hot or cold.

1 teaspoon yellow mustard seeds
2 pounds, 12 ounces yellow bell peppers
2 pounds, 12 ounces red bell peppers
¾ cup cider vinegar

1½ cups granulated sugar
¼ small Thai chili, seeded and finely chopped

MAKES ABOUT: 3 pounds, 8 ounces (5½ cups) PREPARATION TIME: 30 minutes, plus 1 month maturing
COOKING TIME: 30 minutes

1 Put the mustard seeds in a nonstick skillet and dry-fry, tossing continuously, about 1 minute until lightly browned. Set to one side.

2 Cut the peppers in half and remove the core and seeds. Thinly slice the flesh and cut into 1-inch pieces.

3 Put the vinegar and sugar in a preserving pan and slowly bring to a boil, stirring until the sugar has dissolved. Reduce the heat and boil gently about 5 minutes until the mixture has reduced by a third.

4 Add the mustard seeds, sliced bell peppers and chili, reduce the heat, and boil rapidly about

20 minutes until the mixture is thick and reduced but the bell peppers still retain their shape.

5 Meanwhile, sterilize enough jars with non-metallic, vinegar-proof lids, or canning jars, so that they are ready to use (see page 14).

6 Spoon the relish into the warmed, sterilized jars. Seal immediately, label and store in a cool, dry, dark place.

7 Let them mature at least 1 month before using. Refrigerate after opening.

Emma's tip Add an Italian note by replacing the mustard seeds with 2 chopped garlic cloves and adding ½ cup raisins to the cooked bell peppers.

Pickles
& Sauces

Spiced Oranges

Spicy orange slices are delicious with roast duck and are remarkably good served with roast chicken, turkey and cold ham, too. The syrup can be used as a glaze when roasting poultry, pork and game.

2 pounds, 4 ounces oranges
1¾ cups white wine vinegar
1¾ cups granulated sugar
3 garlic cloves, finely chopped
1 thin slice of red chili, finely chopped
1 tablespoon whole allspice

5 star anise
½ cinnamon stick
4 teaspoons coriander seeds
2 tablespoons mace blades
8 whole cloves
4 teaspoons black peppercorns

MAKES ABOUT: 2 pounds, 4 ounces (3½ cups) PREPARATION TIME: 30 minutes, plus 2 to 3 hours cooling, 24 hours freezing and 1 month maturing COOKING TIME: 10 minutes

1 Put the oranges in a large, heavy pot and add enough water to cover. Bring to a boil and then remove from the heat and drain well.

2 Put the oranges in a plastic freezer container, let cool 2 to 3 hours, then freeze 24 hours.

3 Meanwhile, put the remaining ingredients in a large, heavy pot. Slowly bring to a boil, stirring until the sugar has dissolved. Remove the pot from the heat, cover and let infuse at room temperature 24 hours.

4 Strain the spiced liquid through cheesecloth into a large, clean pot and discard the contents of the cheesecloth. Return the liquid to a boil, then remove from the heat and let cool a little so you can handle.

5 Sterilize enough straight-sided, wide-necked jars with non-metallic, vinegar-proof lids, or canning jars, so that they are ready to use (see page 14).

6 Cut two-thirds of the frozen oranges into eighths. Slice the remaining oranges into ¼-inch slices.

7 Put the orange slices around the sides of the warmed, sterilized jars and fill the centers with the quartered oranges. If you have extra orange slices left, add them to the center of the jar.

8 When the spiced vinegar is cold, pour it into the jars to cover the oranges. Seal immediately, label and store in a cool, dry, dark place.

9 Let mature at least 1 month before using. Refrigerate after opening.

Pickled Black Grapes

These bunches of spicy, sweet and sour grapes go well with roast chicken, broiled pork chops and sausages. You could also toss them in a chicken salad, or serve with pâté and hot toast for a delicious first course.

1½ cups cider vinegar
1¾ cups light brown sugar
1-inch piece ginger root, peeled and thinly
    sliced

½ teaspoon cardamom pods, bruised
1 cinnamon stick
3 bay leaves
2 pounds, 4 ounces (5½ cups) seedless black grapes

MAKES ABOUT: 2 pounds, 4 ounces (3½ cups)   PREPARATION TIME: 20 minutes, plus 1 hour cooling and
1 week maturing COOKING TIME: 10 minutes

1 Put the vinegar, sugar, ginger, cardamom pods, cinnamon stick and bay leaves in a large, heavy pot. Slowly bring to a boil, stirring until the sugar has dissolved, and boil rapidly about 5 minutes but do not let it turn brown. Let cool at least 1 hour.

2 Sterilize enough wide-necked jars with non-metallic, vinegar-proof lids, or canning jars, so that they are ready to use (see page 14).

3 Remove small bunches of grapes (each with about 5 grapes) from the vine. Put the grape bunches into the warmed, sterilized jars.

4 When the spiced vinegar is cold, pour it into the jars to cover the grapes, adding all the spices. Seal immediately, label and store in a cool, dry, dark place.

5 Let mature 1 week before using. Refrigerate after opening.

Pickled Pears

Often served at Christmas time, and for good reason, as these are an excellent accompaniment to leftover cold turkey and ham. Also try slicing the Pickled Pears and adding to a salad tossed with crispy bacon and walnuts.

2 pounds, 4 ounces pears, peeled, cored
  and quartered
4 cups white wine vinegar
3 cups granulated sugar

grated zest and juice of 1 lemon
2½ teaspoons ginger paste
1 cinnamon stick, broken in half
4 whole cloves

MAKES ABOUT: 2 pounds, 4 ounces (3½ cups)   PREPARATION TIME: 25 minutes, plus 1 month maturing
COOKING TIME: 20 minutes

1 Sterilize enough wide-necked jars with non-metallic, vinegar-proof lids, or canning jars, so that they are ready to use (see page 14).

2 Put the pears in a large, heavy pot, cover with boiling water and bring to a boil. Reduce the heat and simmer about 5 minutes until beginning to soften. Remove from the pot, drain well, and set to one side.

3 Put the vinegar, sugar, lemon zest and juice, ginger paste, cinnamon stick and cloves in the pot and slowly bring to a boil, stirring until the sugar has

dissolved. Reduce the heat, add the pears and simmer gently about 10 minutes until the pears are tender and translucent. They are ready when the tip of a sharp knife can be inserted easily.

4 Spoon the pears into the warmed, sterilized jars. Add the cinnamon stick pieces and cloves, if you like. Pour in the spiced vinegar to cover the pears. Seal immediately, label and store in a cool, dry, dark place.

5 Let mature at least 1 month before using. Refrigerate after opening.

Emma's tip Cloves in particular continue to impart their distinctive flavor during storage. If you don't like cloves, discard before canning.

Cerises au Vinaigre

In France these spiced, sweet and sour cherries are served with cured and cooked meats, pâtés and Pork Rillettes (see page 218). You could also serve them alongside a bowl of olives to accompany drinks.

2 pounds, 4 ounces (5 cups) cherries
1⅓ cups white wine vinegar
2½ cups granulated sugar
1 star anise

½ teaspoon black peppercorns
1 teaspoon coriander seeds
1 cinnamon stick
4 whole cloves

MAKES ABOUT: 2 pounds, 4 ounces (3½ cups) PREPARATION TIME: 25 minutes, plus 1 month maturing
COOKING TIME: 15 minutes

1 Sterilize enough wide-necked jars with non-metallic, vinegar-proof lids, or canning jars, so that they are ready to use (see page 14).

2 Without removing their stalks or pits, prick each cherry with a sewing needle to help them remain plump during cooking.

3 Put the vinegar, sugar, star anise, peppercorns, coriander seeds, cinnamon stick and cloves in a large, heavy pot. Slowly bring to a boil, stirring until the sugar has dissolved. Reduce the heat, add the cherries and simmer very gently 3 to 4 minutes until the cherries are tender but do not let them burst.

4 Using a slotted spoon, put the cherries into the warmed, sterilized jars. Discard the spices.

5 Bring the syrup in the pot to a boil and boil rapidly about 5 minutes until the syrup begins to thicken but do not let it turn brown.

6 Pour the spiced vinegar into the jars to cover the cherries. Seal immediately, label and store in a cool, dry, dark place.

7 Let mature at least 1 month before using. Refrigerate after opening.

Mediterranean Piccalilli

Mediterranean vegetables make this an unusual alternative to the usual piccalilli and would make a lovely summer variation, particularly if you have a good supply of zucchini, peppers and tomatoes. You can serve it hot or cold.

¼ cup olive oil
1 pound, 9 ounces eggplants, cut into bite-size cubes
1 pound, 9 ounces zucchini, sliced
12 ounces (2¾ cups) green bell peppers, cut in half lengthwise, seeded and cut into bite-size pieces
12 ounces (2¾ cups) red bell peppers, cut in half lengthwise, seeded and cut into bite-size cubes
12 ounces (3 cups) onions, roughly chopped
12 ounces (2 cups) tomatoes, roughly chopped

2 garlic cloves, finely chopped
½ cup all-purpose flour
1 teaspoon ground cinnamon
1 teaspoon freshly ground nutmeg
2 tablespoons turmeric
½ teaspoon dried oregano
1 teaspoon ground black pepper
2 teaspoons salt
2½ cups white wine vinegar
heaped ¾ cup granulated sugar

MAKES ABOUT: 3 pounds, 5 ounces (5 cups)   PREPARATION TIME: 40 minutes, plus 1 month maturing
COOKING TIME: 25 minutes

1 Sterilize enough wide-necked jars with non-metallic, vinegar-proof lids, or canning jars, so that they are ready to use (see page 14).

2 Heat the oil in a preserving pan, add the eggplants, zucchini, peppers, onions, tomatoes and garlic and fry about 15 minutes, stirring frequently, until the vegetables are tender. The vegetables should be soft but not mushy.

3 Meanwhile, put the flour, cinnamon, nutmeg, turmeric, oregano, black pepper and salt in a bowl. Add 2 tablespoons of the vinegar and blend together until smooth.

4 Pour the remaining vinegar into the pan. Add the sugar and heat over low heat, stirring until the sugar has dissolved.

5 Stir the spice mixture into the pan. Slowly bring to a boil, stirring all the time and then cook 2 minutes until thickened. Season with salt if necessary.

6 Spoon the piccalilli into the warmed, sterilized jars. Seal immediately, label and store in a cool, dry, dark place.

7 Let mature at least 1 month before using. Refrigerate after opening.

Balsamic Onions

Perfect pop-in-the-mouth-size onions, preserved in a slightly sweet and spicy vinegar. Using balsamic vinegar is more expensive but it adds a lovely rich sweetness.

¼ cup fine salt
2 pounds, 4 ounces small white boiling onions
1½ teaspoons pickling spices

2¾ cups balsamic vinegar
1 thin slice of red chili, finely chopped
½ teaspoon yellow mustard seeds

MAKES ABOUT: 2 pounds, 4 ounces (3½ cups)   PREPARATION TIME: 25 minutes, plus 24 hours curing and 1 month maturing   COOKING TIME: 5 minutes

1 Pour 4 cups water into a large bowl, add the salt and stir until dissolved.

2 Add the onions and let cure 24 hours.

3 Sterilize enough wide-necked jars with non-metallic, vinegar-proof lids, or canning jars, so that they are ready to use (see page 14).

4 Rinse the onions well under cold running water and let drain.

5 Tie the pickling spices in some cheesecloth. Pour the vinegar into a large, heavy pot, add the cheesecloth

bag and chili and heat gently until almost boiling. Remove the pot from the heat.

6 Spoon the onions into the warmed, sterilized jars. Pour in the spiced vinegar to cover the onions. Add the mustard seeds, dividing equally into the jars. Seal immediately, label and store in a cool, dry, dark place.

7 Let mature at least 1 month before using. Refrigerate after opening.

Emma's tip Don't discard the balsamic vinegar marinade when you have eaten the onions, but use it to make salad dressings with extra virgin olive oil. Drizzle it over salad greens, thinly sliced red onions, avocado, oranges and walnuts. A few drops of the marinade can also enhance sliced strawberries and pears, as well as steaks, eggs, broiled fish and cold meats. You can also brush it over broiled chicken breasts to add a glaze.

Sweet Pickled Beets

These are sweet, spiced pickled beets, rather than the usual pickled beets in vinegar. The addition of sugar complements and brings out the beet's natural sweetness. Serve these tasty beets with cold meats, or use sliced in a sandwich or add at the last minute to a duck, beef or chicken salad.

2 pounds, 4 ounces small raw beets
4 cups red wine vinegar
2½ cups granulated sugar
1 bay leaf
1 cinnamon stick

4 whole cloves
¼ teaspoon whole allspice
⅛ teaspoon black peppercorns
1 teaspoon salt

MAKES ABOUT: 2 pounds, 4 ounces (3½ cups) PREPARATION TIME: 25 minutes, plus 1 month maturing
COOKING TIME: 2 hours 5 minutes

1 Trim the beet tops but do not remove the roots or cut into the skin or else the beets will bleed their color during cooking.

2 Put the vinegar and all other ingredients in a preserving pan or large, heavy pot. Slowly bring to a boil, stirring until the sugar has dissolved. Reduce the heat, add the beets and simmer very gently 1½ to 2 hours until the beets are tender.

3 Sterilize enough wide-necked jars with non-metallic, vinegar-proof lids, or canning jars, so that they are ready to use (see page 14).

4 Using a slotted spoon, remove the beets from the pan and let cool.

5 Meanwhile, strain the spiced vinegar through cheesecloth into a large, clean pan and set to one side. Discard the contents of the cheesecloth.

6 When the beets are cool enough to handle (wear disposable plastic gloves to prevent staining your hands), cut off the roots and peel off the skin. Put the beets into the warmed, sterilized jars.

7 Return the spiced vinegar to a boil, then pour it into the jars to cover the beets. Seal immediately, label and store in a cool, dry, dark place.

8 Let mature at least 1 month before using. Refrigerate after opening.

A Peck of Pickled Peppers

Not only a childhood tongue-twister, these colorful peppers are an attractive and delicious addition to salads, roast vegetables and pizzas. They will also liven up a ham or chicken sandwich and, chopped and mixed with a little mayonnaise, they make a good spread to serve on triangles of toasted bread.

2 red bell peppers
2 yellow bell peppers
2 green bell peppers
2½ cups white wine vinegar
1½ cups granulated sugar
4 garlic cloves

4 whole cloves
2 bay leaves
½ teaspoon black peppercorns
2 teaspoons whole coriander seeds
1 teaspoon salt

MAKES ABOUT: 1 pound, 4 ounces (2 cups)   PREPARATION TIME: 20 minutes, plus 1 week maturing
COOKING TIME: 15 minutes

1 Cut the peppers in half lengthwise, remove the core and seeds, and cut the flesh into ⅝-inch slices.

2 Sterilize enough wide-necked jars with non-metallic, vinegar-proof lids, or canning jars, so that they are ready to use (see page 14).

3 Put all the remaining ingredients except the peppers in a large, heavy pot. Slowly bring to a boil, stirring until the sugar has dissolved. Reduce the heat, add the peppers and simmer gently about 10 minutes until the peppers are just tender.

4 Using a slotted spoon, put the peppers into the warmed, sterilized jars.

5 Add the bay leaves and spices to the jars and pour in the spiced vinegar to cover the peppers completely. Seal immediately, label and store in a cool, dry, dark place.

6 Let mature at least 1 week before using. Refrigerate after opening.

Pickled Garlic Relish

This sweet, punchy relish has a chutney-like consistency. Serve it with a curry, or add a spoonful to sauces, stir-fries or roasted vegetables. You can also serve it spread thinly on toasted bread or bagels on its own or topped with something savory to serve with drinks.

9 ounces garlic bulbs (about 3 large whole heads)
½ cup white wine vinegar
1¾ cups granulated sugar
2 tablespoons lemon juice
⅓ cup sunflower oil
4 teaspoons brown mustard seeds

4 teaspoons cumin seeds
1 teaspoon cayenne pepper
2 teaspoons ground fenugreek
½ teaspoon turmeric
1 teaspoon salt

MAKES ABOUT: 1 pound, 10 ounces (2½ cups) PREPARATION TIME: 30 minutes, plus 1 week maturing
COOKING TIME: 20 minutes

1 Sterilize enough small, wide-necked jars with non-metallic, vinegar-proof lids, or canning jars, so that they are ready to use (see page 14).

2 Break the garlic bulbs into individual cloves and peel each one. Put in a food processor and roughly chop.

3 Put the vinegar and sugar in a large, heavy pot. Slowly bring to a boil, stirring until the sugar has dissolved.

4 Reduce the heat, add the chopped garlic and all the remaining ingredients and simmer gently about

15 minutes until the mixture is thick but still with a little liquid in the bottom of the pot. Stir from time to time to prevent the mixture from sticking to the bottom of the pot.

5 Spoon the relish into the warmed, sterilized jars. Seal immediately, label and store in a cool, dry, dark place.

6 Let mature at least 1 week before using. Refrigerate after opening.

Emma's tip Be very careful towards the end of cooking that the relish does not become too thick, as it gets thicker as it cools and can easily become too sticky.

Horseradish

The traditional accompaniment to roast beef and smoked fish—they aren't the same without it. Be careful not to touch your eyes while preparing the horseradish since it can really sting, and wash your hands well in warm soapy water after you have grated it.

1 teaspoon salt
8 ounces horseradish root
2 cups distilled white vinegar
1 bay leaf
12 peppercorns
1 tablespoon granulated sugar

TO SERVE
1 teaspoon prepared English mustard
¼ cup heavy cream
1 teaspoon granulated sugar
salt and freshly ground black pepper

MAKES ABOUT: 8 ounces (1 cup) PREPARATION TIME: 20 minutes COOKING TIME: 10 minutes

1 Sterilize enough small, wide-necked jars with non-metallic, vinegar-proof lids, or canning jars, so that they are ready to use (see page 14).

2 Fill a large bowl with 2½ cups boiling water and add the salt. Peel and grate the horseradish right into the water to prevent it from turning brown.

3 Drain the horseradish well and pat dry with paper towels. Put into the warmed, sterilized jars, filling them two thirds full.

4 Pour the vinegar into a pot and add the bay leaf, peppercorns and sugar. Bring to a boil, then reduce the heat and simmer 5 minutes.

5 Strain the vinegar through a strainer and pour into the jars to cover the horseradish. Seal immediately, label and store in a cool, dry, dark place. Refrigerate after opening.

6 To serve, spoon 3 tablespoons of the horseradish and 2 teaspoons of vinegar from the jar, into a bowl. Add the mustard, cream and sugar and stir together. Season to taste with salt and pepper.

Cranberry & Orange Sauce

Also known as Cranberry and Orange Marmalade, this is a tangy, refreshing accompaniment with a vibrant color. It is a versatile sauce—stir a spoonful into gravy for color and extra flavor, or serve alongside roast turkey, chicken, goose or duck. It is also delicious with brie and a baguette.

2 oranges
1 pound, 2 ounces (5½ cups) cranberries

2½ cups granulated sugar

MAKES ABOUT: 2 pounds, 4 ounces (3½ cups) PREPARATION TIME: 25 minutes, plus 2 weeks maturing
COOKING TIME: 55 minutes

1 Cut the oranges in half and squeeze out the juice and seeds. Slice the orange peel with its pith into thin shreds, about 1½-inches long.

2 Put the peel, orange juice and 4 cups water into a large, heavy pot and slowly bring to a boil. Reduce the heat and simmer gently about 30 minutes until the peel is really soft and the liquid reduced by about a third.

3 Meanwhile, sterilize enough small, wide-necked jars in the oven so that they are ready to use (see page 14).

4 Add the cranberries to the pot, return to a boil, reduce the heat and simmer 10 to 15 minutes until soft and the skins burst.

5 Reduce the heat, add the sugar to the pot and stir until completely dissolved. Return to a boil and boil 3 minutes.

6 Spoon the sauce into the warmed, sterilized jars and cover immediately with sterilized lids. Label and store in a cool, dry, dark place.

7 Let mature at least 2 weeks before using. Refrigerate after opening.

Emma's tip Fresh cranberries are only in season in the fall but you can use frozen cranberries instead. It is not necessary to thaw them before using it. If you like ginger, you could grate a small piece of ginger root and add with the cranberries.

Bramley Applesauce

This versatile British everyday applesauce is delicious served with roast pork, broiled pork chops, duck or with sausage and mashed potato. You can also serve it as a dessert, or add a spoonful to your breakfast cereal or oatmeal, sprinkled with a dusting of ground cinnamon.

juice of 1 lemon
2 pounds, 4 ounces Bramley or other cooking apples

¼ cup granulated sugar
2 tablespoons butter

MAKES ABOUT: 1 pound, 9 ounces (2 cups) PREPARATION TIME: 30 minutes, plus canning (optional) COOKING TIME: 20 minutes

1 Sterilize enough canning jars so that they are ready to use (see page 14). Otherwise, you can store the sauce in plastic containers in the freezer.

2 Pour ⅔ cup water into a large, heavy pot and add the lemon juice.

3 Peel, core and cut the apples into chunks and add to the pot as you prepare them to prevent them from turning brown.

4 Sprinkle the sugar over the apples. Bring to a boil, reduce the heat, cover with a lid, and simmer gently about 15 minutes until the apples are very soft. Stir from time to time to prevent the mixture from sticking to the bottom of the pot.

5 If you prefer a rough textured sauce, beat the mixture well with a wooden spoon until it is the texture you want. If you prefer a smooth sauce, put the softened apples in a food processor and blend until smooth. Return the applesauce to the pot.

6 Add the butter and heat very gently until melted. Stir all the time to prevent the applesauce from sticking to the bottom of the pot.

7 Spoon the applesauce into the warmed, sterilized jars, leaving a ½-inch gap between the top of the sauce and the lid. Tap the jars lightly on the counter to remove any air bubbles. Fit the sterilized rubber band or metal lid and seal the jars. If using screw-band jars, loosen by a quarter-turn after sealing. Label and store in a cool, dry, dark place.

8 Alternatively, pour the applesauce into plastic freezer containers and label. Let cool and then seal and store in the freezer. Let thaw at room temperature about 8 hours before serving.

9 Serve cold or, to serve hot, reheat the sauce gently in a pot. Once opened, store the sauce in the refrigerator and eat within 1 week.

Mint Sauce

A mandatory accompaniment to roast lamb! It is also the perfect solution to what to do with all that mint should you have it growing in your garden, since it has a tendency to grow rather freely.

⅔ cup white wine vinegar
heaped ½ cup granulated sugar

3½ ounces (6 to 7 cups) mint leaves
a pinch of salt

MAKES ABOUT: 5fl oz (⅔ cup) PREPARATION TIME: 25 minutes, plus 2 to 3 hours cooling
COOKING TIME: 2 minutes

1 Put the vinegar and sugar in a large, heavy pot. Slowly bring to a boil, stirring until the sugar has dissolved. Remove the pot from the heat and let cool 2 to 3 hours.

2 Sterilize a small, wide-necked jar with a non-metallic, vinegar-proof lid, so that it is ready to use (see page 14).

3 Strip the mint leaves off their stalks and chop fine. Put the chopped mint in a bowl and pour some hot water over it to set the color of the mint. Drain well and pat dry on paper towels. Sprinkle with salt and put the mint into the warmed, sterilized jar.

4 When the vinegar is cold, pour it into the jar to cover the mint. Seal immediately, label and store in a cool, dry, dark place.

5 To serve the sauce, spoon out the amount of sauce that you'd like along with a little of the vinegar into a gravy boat or bowl.

Emma's tip It can be a laborious task but, when you remove the mint leaves from their stems, try not to include any stems as these can add bitterness to the sauce. It is also a good idea to sprinkle a few teaspoons of the sugar over the mint leaves before chopping since this helps to extract the mint's oils and also provides the knife with a rough texture, which helps to finely chop the mint.

Honey Barbecue Sauce

Sweetened and flavored with honey, this sauce is wonderful basted over barbecued meats, such as pork spareribs and chicken drumsticks, or simply serve a spoonful alongside barbecued hot dogs, sausages and burgers.

1 tablespoon olive oil
18 ounces (4 to 4½ cups) onions, finely chopped
2¼ cups tomato passata
⅓ cup honey
3 tablespoons balsamic vinegar

2 tablespoons soy sauce
1 tablespoon ginger paste
½ teaspoon salt
½ teaspoon ground black pepper

MAKES ABOUT: 1 quart PREPARATION TIME: 25 minutes, plus canning (optional) COOKING TIME: 45 minutes

1 Sterilize enough wide-necked bottles in the oven so that they are ready to use (see page 14). If using screw-top bottles with metal lids, fit the lids with cut-out discs of wax paper to prevent the sauce coming in contact with the metal.

2 Heat the oil in a large, heavy pot. Add the onions and fry gently about 15 minutes, stirring occasionally, until softened and starting to turn brown.

3 Add all the remaining ingredients and bring to a boil. Reduce the heat and simmer 20 to 30 minutes until reduced and thickened.

4 Transfer the mixture to a food processor or blender, and blend until smooth. Return the mixture to the pot and heat gently until hot.

5 Using a funnel, pour the sauce into the warmed, sterilized bottles, leaving a ½-inch gap between the top of the sauce and the lid. Fit the sterilized rubber band or metal lid and seal the bottle. If using a screw-band bottle, loosen by a quarter-turn after sealing. Label and store in the refrigerator. Eat within 3 months.

6 If you wish to store the sauce for longer, follow the instructions for canning on page 23.

Emma's tip You can preserve the sauce by freezing, if you prefer. Pour the sauce into clean, plastic bottles, leaving a 1-inch head-space to allow for expansion. Label and freeze. Let the sauce thaw at room temperature about 8 hours before serving. Keep in the refrigerator once opened.

Wholegrain Honey Mustard

Everyone needs a small supply of wholegrain mustard and this one is very easy to make. Serve a spoonful with broiled steaks, spread on your cheese sandwich, or add to dressings and marinades. Its uses are endless!

⅓ cup yellow mustard seeds
3 tablespoons black mustard seeds
½ cup cider vinegar
2 tablespoons honey

½ teaspoon ground ginger
½ teaspoon ground cinnamon
½ teaspoon salt

MAKES ABOUT: 1 cup   PREPARATION TIME: 15 minutes, plus 24 hours soaking and 1 week maturing

1 Put the yellow and black mustard seeds in a bowl and add the vinegar. Cover and let soak at room temperature 24 hours.

2 Sterilize a small, wide-necked jar with a non-metallic, vinegar-proof lid, so that it is ready to use (see page 14).

3 Put three quarters of the soaked mustard seeds in a food processor and blend, using a pulsating action, until a thick paste has formed. This will take several minutes. Transfer to a bowl.

4 Add the honey, ginger, cinnamon and salt to the mixture and blend together until well combined.

5 Add the reserved soaked seeds to the mixture and stir together.

6 Pack the mixture into the warmed, sterilized jar. Seal immediately, label and store in a cool, dry, dark place.

7 Let mature at least 1 week before using. Refrigerate after opening.

Tomato Ketchup

Loved by adults as well as children, this homemade Tomato Ketchup is less sweet than many commercial products. It is very simple to make, and a useful way to use up a bumper crop of tomatoes each year.

1 tablespoon olive oil

2 red onions, chopped

2 garlic cloves, finely chopped

2 pounds, 4 ounces (5 to 6 cups) tomatoes, skinned (see page 48) and roughly chopped

2 tablespoons tomato paste

⅓ cup light brown sugar

1 scant cup red wine vinegar

1 teaspoon paprika

½ teaspoon mustard powder

¼ teaspoon ground cloves

2 bay leaves

½ teaspoon salt

½ teaspoon ground black pepper

MAKES ABOUT: 1 quart   PREPARATION TIME: 20 minutes   COOKING TIME: 30 to 45 minutes

1 Sterilize enough bottles in the oven so that they are ready to use (see page 14). If using screw-top bottles with metal lids, fit the lids with cut-out wax-paper discs to prevent the ketchup coming in contact with the metal.

2 Heat the oil in a large, heavy pot. Add the onions and fry gently 10 to 15 minutes, stirring occasionally, until softened and starting to turn brown.

3 Add the garlic and fry 1 minute. Add all the remaining ingredients and bring to a boil. Reduce the heat and simmer 20 to 30 minutes until reduced and thickened.

4 Remove the bay leaves from the pot. Put the mixture into a food processor or blender and blend until smooth. Return the mixture to the pot and heat gently until hot.

5 Using a funnel, pour the ketchup into the warmed, sterilized bottles, leaving a ½-inch gap between the top of the sauce and the lid. Fit the sterilized rubber band or metal lid and seal the bottle. If using a screw-band bottle, loosen by a quarter-turn after sealing. Label and store in the refrigerator. Eat within 3 months.

6 If you wish to store the ketchup for longer, follow the instructions for canning on page 23.

7 Once opened, store the ketchup in the refrigerator.

Emma's tip You can use canned tomatoes if you need a new supply of ketchup later in the year. Replace the fresh tomatoes with 2 x 14½-ounce cans chopped tomatoes. If using canned tomatoes, there is no need to include the tomato paste in the recipe, which is added to the fresh tomatoes to enhance the color of the ketchup.

Mushroom Ketchup

Dating further back than Tomato Ketchup, Mushroom Ketchup used to include fish. This recipe uses delicious spices to add flavor instead, and has been given a modern slant by making it a thicker ketchup to serve with broiled and barbecued foods, rather than the thin dark mushroom ketchup used as a cooking ingredient.

2 pounds, 4 ounces large wide-capped or wild mushrooms, sliced
3 tablespoons fine salt
2 shallots, quartered
2 garlic cloves
1¼ cups cider vinegar
heaped ½ cup dark brown sugar

1 teaspoon ground allspice
¼ teaspoon ground ginger
½ teaspoon ground cloves
¼ teaspoon ground cinnamon
½ teaspoon ground mace
½ teaspoon paprika

MAKES ABOUT: 2½ to 3 cups PREPARATION TIME: 35 minutes, plus 12 hours or overnight standing, 2 weeks maturing and canning (optional) COOKING TIME: 1 hour

1 Put the mushrooms in a large bowl and sprinkle the salt over them. Cover and leave in a cool place 12 hours or overnight. This will darken the mushrooms.

2 The next day, rinse the mushrooms under cold running water and drain well.

3 Put the mushrooms in a food processor and add the shallots and garlic. Blend to form a puree. Transfer the puree to a large, heavy pot.

4 Add the vinegar and sugar to the pot and heat gently, stirring until the sugar dissolves. Add all the remaining ingredients, bring to a boil, reduce the heat, and simmer about 1 hour until no excess liquid remains and the mixture is thick. Stir from time to time to prevent the mixture from sticking to the bottom of the pot.

5 Sterilize enough wide-necked bottles so that they are ready to use (see page 14). If using screw-top bottles with metal lids, fit the lids with cut-out wax-paper discs to prevent the ketchup coming in contact with the metal.

6 Using a funnel, pour the ketchup into the warmed, sterilized bottles, leaving a ½-inch gap between the top of the sauce and the lid. Fit the sterilized rubber band or metal lid and seal the bottle. If using a screw-band bottle, loosen by a quarter-turn after sealing. Label and store in the refrigerator. Let mature at least 2 weeks before using. Eat within 3 months.

7 If you wish to store the ketchup for longer, follow the instructions for canning on page 23.

Candied, Cured, Dried & Canned

Candied Ginger

Serve these delicate, sweet pieces of ginger with coffee, as you would chocolates, or they also make a wonderful addition to cupcakes, cookies, muffins, ice cream and even your morning bowl of oatmeal.

9 ounces ginger root, peeled
1¼ cups granulated sugar

heaped ½ cup superfine sugar

MAKES ABOUT: 10 ounces   PREPARATION TIME: 35 minutes, plus 1 hour cooling and 24 hours drying
COOKING TIME: 55 minutes

1 Using a sharp knife, a mandoline or the slicing attachment of a food processor, thinly slice the ginger.

2 Put the ginger slices into a large, heavy pot. Pour in enough cold water to just cover the ginger, bring to a boil, reduce the heat, simmer 10 minutes then drain and discard the water. Repeat the procedure one more time, but reserve the liquid. Measure the liquid to make up to 1 cup. Add more water, if necessary.

3 Pour the liquid into the pot, add the granulated sugar and heat gently, stirring, until the sugar has dissolved. Add the ginger slices, bring to a boil, reduce the heat and simmer gently about 30 minutes until the ginger is tender and transparent.

4 Remove the pot from the heat and let cool at least 1 hour. When the ginger pieces are cold, drain well.

5 Put a wire rack over a baking tray. Spread the superfine sugar onto a large plate and coat each piece of ginger with superfine sugar. Put the sugar-coated ginger on the wire rack and sprinkle any remaining sugar over the top.

6 Let the ginger dry at room temperature for 24 hours.

7 Store the ginger in a non-airtight wood or cardboard box, between layers of wax paper, keeping each piece separate, in a cool, dry place.

Emma's tip If you like you can preserve the ginger in the syrup. Sterilize enough small jars in the oven so that they are ready to use (see page 14). Spoon the ginger slices into the jars and pour the syrup over them to cover the ginger. Leave a ½-inch gap between the top of the liquid and lid. Label and store in the refrigerator. Eat within 1 month.

Chocolate-Dipped Candied Citrus Peel

Serve with after-dinner coffee or package it to give as a present. You could also make a batch without chocolate to use chopped in cakes, cookies and plum puddings; it will taste far superior to the commercially prepared candied peel.

2 thick-skinned oranges
1 lemon
1 heaped cup granulated sugar

heaped ½ cup superfine sugar
3 ounces bittersweet chocolate (70% cocoa solids), broken into small pieces

MAKES ABOUT: 68 pieces PREPARATION TIME: 45 minutes, plus 1 hour cooling, 24 hours drying and 1 to 2 hours setting COOKING TIME: 45 minutes

1 Cut the oranges and lemon in half widthwise and then in half lengthwise. Using a sharp knife, remove the flesh.

2 Cut each orange skin into about 6 slices, and the lemon skins into about 5 slices each, making triangular shapes.

3 Put the peels into a large, heavy pot. Pour in enough cold water to just cover the peels, bring to a boil and then drain. Repeat the procedure four more times. The final time, drain the peel well and set it aside, and reserve 1 cup of the water.

4 Pour the reserved water into the pot, add the granulated sugar and heat gently, stirring, until the sugar has dissolved. Add the orange and lemon peel, bring to a boil, reduce the heat and simmer gently about 40 minutes until the syrup has almost evaporated and the peel is tender and transparent. Remove the pot from the heat and let cool at least 1 hour.

5 Put a wire rack over a baking tray. When cool, drain the peel well.

6 Spread the superfine sugar onto a large plate and coat each piece of peel with the superfine sugar. Put the sugar-coated peel on the wire rack and sprinkle any remaining sugar over the top.

7 Let the peel dry at room temperature 24 hours.

8 Line a baking tray with wax paper. Put the chocolate in the top of a double boiler set over boiling water. Stir occasionally until the chocolate has melted. Remove the double-boiler from the heat.

9 Dip the flat ends of the candied peel into the melted chocolate, then put them on the lined baking tray. Leave them 1 to 2 hours until set.

10 Put the candied peel in a non-airtight wood or cardboard box, between layers of wax paper, keeping each piece separate. Store in a cool, dry place.

Dried Chili Wreath

Strings of chilies, known as *ristra*, are seen everywhere in New Mexico where the traditional method of preserving chili pods is air-drying. Not only is it useful to have a supply of chilies to crumble into recipes, but the wreath also looks attractive as a decoration in the home. If you do not have dried bay leaves, you could use twists of raffia instead.

22-inch strong but flexible wire, such as a
    coat hanger

about 30 firm, red chilies
about 30 dried bay leaves, optional

MAKES: 1 wreath PREPARATION TIME: 45 minutes, plus 2 weeks drying

1 Wear thin plastic gloves to protect your hands. Thread the wire through the top of the first chili stem. Then thread it through a dried bay leaf, if using, followed closely by the next chili. Continue until you have threaded all the chilies and bay leaves together. Push the chilies close enough together so that you don't see the wire.

2 Wind the ends of the wire together to make a circle.

3 If the sun is shining, hang the wreath in the sun during the day for 2 weeks, putting it in a warm draft-free place at night. Alternatively, hang in a warm draft-free place the whole time. Turn the chilies occasionally to ensure even drying.

4 When dried, hang the wreath in a cool, dry place. Use as required.

Emma's tip Bunches of herbs can be dried and displayed in the same way. Tie thick bunches of bay leaves, sage, rosemary and thyme with thread. Attach to a wire circle, as explained above, overlapping each bunch so that the stems and wire are hidden.

Dried Herbs

A supply of dried herbs is useful to add to the cooking pot in the winter months, when fresh herbs are not in season. Pick herbs before they flower on a dry day after the dew has gone.

bunches of fresh herbs, such as rosemary, bay leaves, sage, marjoram, parsley or mint

PREPARATION TIME: 15 minutes, plus 3 to 5 days drying

1 Wash the herbs if you like, but it is not essential. Dry on paper towels. Dip parsley and mint in a pot of boiling water 1 minute to retain their color.

2 Tie the herbs in bunches using string and put in a paper bag, with their heads down and stalks protruding. Tie the ends of the string around the neck of the bag.

3 Hang the herbs upside down in a warm, dry place. Leave them 3 to 5 days until the leaves are dry and rub off their stalks easily.

4 Put the bay leaves in an airtight container. Crumble the other herbs before storing in airtight containers.

5 Store in a cool, dark place for up to 1 year. Use as needed.

Emma's tip To make the classic dried herb mixture *Herbes de Provence,* mix together equal quantities of dried basil, marjoram, oregano, rosemary, sage, savory and thyme.

Bouquets Garnis

Useful throughout the year for flavoring soups, stocks and stews, you can adapt your Bouquets Garnis according to which herbs you grow. This is a classic combination.

1 bay leaf sprig
4 thyme stalks

2 rosemary sprigs
2 parsley stalks

MAKES: 1 Bouquet Garni PREPARATION TIME: 15 minutes, plus 3 days drying

1 Tie the herbs together with string, put in a paper bag and dry as above. Make as many as you like.

2 Leave about 3 days until dried. Put them in cheesecloth squares and tie with string.

3 Store the bundles in an airtight jar in a cool, dark place for up to 1 year. Use as needed.

Dried Apple Rings

The traditional method of drying fruits is in the sun but, since the weather cannot always be relied upon, this recipe uses the more reliable method of using your oven.

⅓ cup lemon juice
1 teaspoon granulated sugar

2 pounds, 4 ounces unblemished, just-ripe
   eating apples
sunflower oil (optional)

MAKES ABOUT: 8 ounces PREPARATION TIME: 35 minutes, plus 11 to 15 hours drying

1 Preheat the oven to its lowest setting, no higher than 225°F.

2 Fill a large bowl with 2½ cups water and add the lemon juice and sugar.

3 Peel, if you like, and core one apple at a time. Slice into rings about ¼-inch thick and add to the lemon water as you prepare, to prevent them from going brown. Leave them 5 minutes and then dry on paper towels.

4 Thread the apple rings onto long thin metal skewers or wooden sticks and place across roasting pans.

Alternatively, brush wire racks with a little sunflower oil and put the apples on the racks in a single layer.

5 Put the apple rings in the oven with the door ajar. Let dry 8 to 12 hours. When dry, turn off the oven and leave the apple rings inside about 3 hours until cold.

6 Put the dried apple rings in a non-airtight wood or cardboard box, between layers of wax paper, keeping each piece separate. Store in a cool, dry place.

Emma's tip Pears can be dried in the same way but should be cut into quarters, instead of rings, and put on wire racks.

Moroccan Preserved Lemons

Expensive to buy, yet so simple to make, Moroccan Preserved Lemons are an essential ingredient in authentic chicken and lamb tagines. They add an appetizing sweet and sour taste that also works well in salads.

6 lemons
heaped ⅓ cup coarse salt
2 red chilies

2 bay leaves
2 star anise
2 tablespoons olive oil

MAKES: 6   PREPARATION TIME: 30 minutes, plus 1 week curing and 1 month maturing

1 Sterilize a 1-quart canning jar so that it is ready to use (see page 14).

2 Cut the lemons lengthwise as if cutting them into quarters, but leaving about 1 inch at the bottom so that they are still in one piece. Open them out slightly and stuff the salt in the centers. Pack into the warmed, sterilized jar so that they fit tightly together.

3 Seal the jar and let cure at room temperature 1 week.

4 Using the end of a wooden spoon, press the lemons to release as much juice as possible.

5 Add the chilies, bay leaves and star anise to the jar. Pour in the oil to cover in a thin layer. Seal, label and let mature at least 1 month before using. Refrigerate after opening.

Emma's tip To use a preserved lemon, cut into quarters, then remove and discard the flesh. Rinse the rind under cold running water to get rid of some of the salt, pat dry, and slice or chop the rind before adding to a tagine or salad.

Harissa Paste

This hot, red, chili sauce is from North Africa and is the perfect partner to tagines, couscous and soups. Harissa Paste is made in small quantities because, with its fiery taste, a little goes a long way.

1¾ ounces red chilies
9 ounces tomatoes, quartered
1 teaspoon ground cumin
1 teaspoon ground coriander
2 teaspoons caraway seeds

4 garlic cloves
1 tablespoon lemon juice
¼ cup extra virgin olive oil, plus
   extra for covering
½ teaspoon salt

MAKES ABOUT: 6 ounces (⅔ cup) PREPARATION TIME: 30 minutes COOKING TIME: 20 minutes

1 Sterilize a small, wide-necked jar with a non-metallic, vinegar-proof lid so that it is ready to use (see page 14).

2 Cut the chilies in half lengthwise and remove the core and seeds with a teaspoon. Keep the seeds if you want to add extra heat.

3 Put the chilies and remaining ingredients in a food processor. Add all or some of the chili seeds if you like a fiery, hot taste. Using a pulsating action, blend the ingredients together to form a paste.

4 Transfer the mixture to a heavy pot. Slowly bring to a boil then reduce the heat and simmer 15 minutes, stirring frequently, until the mixture is thick and no excess liquid remains in the bottom of the pot.

5 Spoon the paste into the warmed, sterilized jar, leaving a ½-inch gap at the top. Pour a little olive oil over the top to cover the mixture and form a thin layer, seal immediately and label.

6 Let cool completely before storing in the refrigerator up to 4 months.

7 Once opened, cover the sauce with a layer of oil before returning it to the refrigerator.

Thai Curry Paste

An essential ingredient in so many curry recipes, it is useful to have a jar of this tucked in the refrigerator. You can also make Red Thai Curry Paste, which is hotter due to the red chilies packing a more powerful punch.

5 green chilies
1 shallot, quartered
½-inch piece ginger root, peeled and roughly chopped
3 garlic cloves
2 lemongrass stalks, chopped

1 teaspoon shrimp paste
1 ounce (1½ cups) cilantro leaves
grated zest and juice of ½ lime
¼ teaspoon salt
¼ teaspoon ground black pepper
extra virgin olive oil, for covering

MAKES ABOUT: 5 ounces (½ cup)   PREPARATION TIME: 30 minutes

1 Sterilize a small, wide-necked jar with a non-metallic, vinegar-proof lid so that it is ready to use (see page 14).

2 Cut the chilies in half and remove the core and seeds with a teaspoon. Keep the seeds to add extra heat, if you like.

3 Put the chilies, shallot, ginger, garlic and lemongrass in a food processor and, using a pulsating action, blend until the ingredients are finely chopped.

4 Add the remaining ingredients, including the chili seeds, if using, and continue blending the mixture together until a thick paste is formed.

5 Spoon the paste into the warmed, sterilized jar, leaving a ½-inch gap at the top. Pour a little olive oil over the top to cover the mixture and form a thin layer. Seal immediately and label.

6 Let cool completely before storing in the refrigerator. The paste will keep for up to 2 weeks. Once opened, cover the paste with a layer of oil before returning it to the refrigerator.

Emma's tip To make Red Thai Curry Paste follow the recipe as above, but replace the green chilies with 4 red chilies. You need a little less garlic, too—2 cloves will be enough.

Korean Kimchi

Sometimes spelled "Kimchee", this is Korea's national dish. There are hundreds of variations of these fermented vegetables but cabbage is most popularly used. It is served as an accompaniment as well as being used as an ingredient in many Korean dishes such as soups, stews and fried rice. Traditionally made by burying a crockpot in the ground, this is a quicker version.

1 pound, 2 ounces Chinese cabbage
3 tablespoons coarse salt
4 garlic cloves, finely chopped
2-inch piece ginger root, peeled and grated
8 scallions, finely sliced

2 to 3 tablespoons chili powder, according to taste
½ cup rice vinegar
¼ cup Thai fish sauce
2 teaspoons granulated sugar

MAKES ABOUT: 1 quart PREPARATION TIME: 25 minutes, plus 12 hours or overnight curing, 24 to 48 hours fermenting and 48 hours maturing

1 Cut the Chinese cabbage lengthwise into quarters and then widthwise into 2-inch slices. Put the cabbage in a large bowl and sprinkle the salt over it. Add enough cold water to just cover the cabbage. Cover the bowl and leave it in a cool place for 8 hours or overnight.

2 Rinse well under cold running water and drain well.

3 Sterilize a 1-quart canning jar so that it is ready to use (see page 14).

4 Put all the ingredients, except the cabbage, into a bowl and mix together well. Add the cabbage and mix well until it's coated in the mixture.

5 Pack the cabbage into the warmed, sterilized jar, pressing it down to let the cabbage release its juices, until the liquid rises to cover the cabbage. Leave a ½-inch gap between the top of the liquid and the lid. Seal and let ferment in a warm place for 24 hours. The mixture may start to bubble which means it is fermenting and is ready; if not, leave it another 24 hours.

6 Open the jar and let the gases escape. Reseal the jar and put in the refrigerator for 48 hours before eating. Serve, or store in the refrigerator and eat within 2 weeks.

Red Bell Pepper & Olive Tapenade

This is a version of the well-known Mediterranean spread but with red bell peppers instead of anchovies. Serve it in the traditional way with French bread and a selection of crudités for dipping. You can also add a spoonful to freshly cooked pasta or boiled new potatoes, or use it to make a salad dressing.

1½ cups pitted Kalamata olives
scant ½ cup capers, drained and rinsed
2 tablespoons olive oil, plus extra for covering
2 pounds, 4 ounces red bell peppers, cut in half lengthwise, seeded and cubed

4 garlic cloves, finely chopped
¼ cup balsamic vinegar
¼ cup sun-dried tomato paste
2 tablespoons dried oregano
1 teaspoon ground black pepper

MAKES ABOUT: 1 pound, 2 ounces (2 cups) PREPARATION TIME: 25 minutes COOKING TIME: 15 minutes

1 Sterilize a wide-necked jar with a non-metallic, vinegar-proof lid, or canning jar, so that it is ready to use (see page 14).

2 Put the olives and capers in a food processor and blend to form a paste. Set to one side.

3 Heat the oil in a large, heavy pot. Add the peppers and garlic and fry gently 10 to 15 minutes, stirring occasionally, until the peppers are just soft.

4 Add the pepper and garlic mixture and all the remaining ingredients to the capers and olives in the food processor. Using a pulsating action, blend until a rough paste is formed. If you prefer a smooth-textured paste, blend until smooth.

5 Spoon the mixture into the warmed, sterilized jar, leaving a ½-inch gap at the top. Pour a little olive oil over the top to cover the mixture and form a thin layer. Seal immediately and label.

6 Let cool completely before storing in the refrigerator for up to 2 weeks. Once opened, cover the paste with a thin layer of olive oil before returning it to the refrigerator.

Goat Cheese in Olive Oil

Keeping cheese in oil excludes air and prolongs the freshness of the cheese. The other advantage is that the oil and herbs impart a wonderful flavor to the goat cheese. Delicious served with salad for a light lunch or snack.

4 x 5-ounce soft goat cheese logs, cut in half
 widthwise
2 rosemary sprigs
2 bay leaves

2 garlic cloves
2 teaspoons black peppercorns
1½ cups extra virgin olive oil

SERVES: 8 PREPARATION TIME: 15 minutes, plus 1 week marinating

1 Sterilize a 1-quart canning jar so that it is ready to use (see page 14).

2 Put the cheese in the warmed, sterilized jar. Add the rosemary sprigs, bay leaves, garlic cloves and peppercorns. Pour in the oil so that it just covers the cheese.

3 Seal the jar and let marinate in the refrigerator 1 week before using. Store in the refrigerator up to 1 week.

4 Serve with a little of the oil drizzled over the top of the cheese.

Emma's tip Any leftover oil can be used in a salad dressing, for drizzling over broiled meat or fish, or as a dip for French bread. It can also be used again to marinate more goat cheese.

Sweet Cured Herrings

A favorite dish from the Nordic countries, particularly Denmark, where they are eaten as an appetizer with rye bread or crispbreads, or as a light meal with new potatoes, crème fraîche or sour cream and salad, or even right from the jar.

6 herring fillets, scaled and trimmed, cut in half lengthwise
1 cup coarse salt
1¾ cups white wine vinegar
¾ cup granulated sugar

2 bay leaves
½ teaspoon black peppercorns
1 teaspoon juniper berries
½ teaspoon yellow mustard seeds
1 small red onion, thinly sliced

MAKES: 12   PREPARATION TIME: 35 minutes, plus 24 hours curing and 3 days maturing
COOKING TIME: 5 minutes

1 Using tweezers, remove the bones from the herring fillets. You can find small bones by running your fingers along the herrings.

2 Put the herrings, flesh-side up, in a deep, non-metallic dish. Sprinkle the salt over the top of the herrings, cover the dish, and let cure in the refrigerator 24 hours.

3 Meanwhile, pour 1 cup water into a large, heavy pot. Add the vinegar and sugar, slowly and bring to a boil, stirring until the sugar has dissolved. Reduce the heat and simmer 2 minutes. Add the bay leaves, peppercorns, juniper berries and mustard seeds. Pour the mixture into a large measuring cup and leave it in a cold place to infuse.

4 When the herrings have cured, drain off the liquid and pat the herrings dry with paper towels.

5 Sterilize a 1-quart canning jar so that it is ready to use (see page 14).

6 Pack the herrings in layers in the warmed, sterilized jar, layering them with the onion.

7 Pour the vinegar mixture over the herring fillets, covering them completely. Seal the jar and store in the refrigerator 3 days before eating. Store up to 3 weeks.

8 To serve, drain the fillets from the marinade and dry them on paper towels. Serve with some of the onions from the jar.

Beet Gravlax

Authentic Gravlax is a Scandinavian method of preserving salmon by burying and curing it in salt under a weight for at least six weeks, but this is a much quicker method. Traditionally just salt, sugar and dill are used, but beet is added here, which has no preservation properties but looks very pretty. Serve the salmon as an appetizer with rye bread or crispbread, or as a light meal with boiled new potatoes, dill pickles and sour cream. Don't forget to serve with lemon wedges to squeeze over the top.

1 tablespoon black peppercorns
2 tablespoons juniper berries
1 tablespoon coriander seeds
1 pound, 2 ounces ounces raw beets, peeled
   and grated
1¾ ounces dill leaves and stalks, finely chopped

3 tablespoons vodka or aquavit
1 cup coarse salt
⅔ cup Demerara sugar
pared zest of 1 lemon
1 pound, 2 ounces middle-cut salmon, skin on

MAKES: 1 pound, 2 ounces PREPARATION TIME: 45 minutes, plus 4 days curing

1 Finely crush the peppercorns, juniper berries and coriander seeds in a mortar and pestle.

2 Put the crushed spices in a bowl. Add the grated beet, dill, vodka, salt, sugar and lemon zest and mix together.

3 Remove the scales from the salmon and, using tweezers, remove the bones. You can find small bones by running your fingers along the salmon. Put the salmon, flesh-side up, in a large, deep, non-metallic dish.

4 Spread the beet mixture over the top of the salmon and rub it into the flesh.

5 Cover the dish and let it cure in the refrigerator 4 days. Twice a day, rub the mixture into the flesh and pour away any excess juices.

6 After 4 days, scrape off the curing mixture and discard. Pat the salmon dry with paper towels. Store in the refrigerator and eat within 1 week.

Emma's tip To slice the Gravlax, use a very sharp, long, narrow-bladed knife and slice diagonally, as thinly as possible, pulling each slice away from the skin. Greasing the knife with a little oil before you start makes it easier to slice the salmon.

Potted Trout

This is a short-term preserve that uses the method of excluding air and moisture under a layer of clarified butter. You can either store it in one dish or individual dishes and it makes a delicious appetizer or light meal. Serve with brown bread or melba toast.

1 tablespoon olive oil
¾ cup (1½ sticks) unsalted butter
2 fresh trout, about 9 ounces each
juice of ½ lemon

⅛ teaspoon ground mace
⅛ teaspoon paprika
⅛ teaspoon freshly grated nutmeg
salt and freshly ground black pepper

SERVES: 6   PREPARATION TIME: 20 minutes, plus 2 to 3 hours cooling and 2 to 3 hours setting
COOKING TIME: 15 minutes

1 Heat the oil and 2 tablespoons of the butter in a large skillet. Add the trout and fry 5 to 10 minutes, turning once, until cooked. Remove the pan from the heat.

2 Skin and roughly flake the fish with a fork, discarding the bones, and put in a bowl.

3 Add the juices from the pan, along with the lemon juice, mace, paprika and nutmeg to the bowl and mix together. Season to taste with salt and pepper.

4 Turn the mixture into a terrine or six individual ramekin dishes and press down lightly.

5 Melt the remaining butter and leave it 2 to 3 minutes to allow the sediment to settle.

6 Carefully pour the clarified butter over the top of the trout to cover, discarding the sediment. Leave the trout 2 to 3 hours until cool.

7 Put the trout in the refrigerator 2 to 3 hours to set. Store in the refrigerator up to 1 week. Once the seal of butter is broken, eat within 3 days.

8 To serve, leave at room temperature about 30 minutes. Serve right from the terrine or ramekin dishes or, if you like, turn it out onto plates.

Emma's tip Clarified butter has been heated to separate the milk solids and water from the butterfat. The recipe explains how to make clarified butter but you can use ⅔ cup ghee instead if you prefer to buy ready-made.

Anchoïade

Serve this classic Provençal paste spread on thin slices of toasted French bread or as a dip with raw vegetables such as carrots, celery, cucumber, fennel, snow peas and bell peppers. Perfect with drinks before a meal.

2 x 2-ounce cans anchovies in olive oil
2 garlic cloves
1 shallot, quartered
8 pitted black olives

1 tablespoon lemon juice
2 tablespoons chopped parsley leaves
extra virgin olive oil, to cover
freshly ground black pepper

MAKES ABOUT: 6 ounces (1 cup) PREPARATION TIME: 15 minutes

1 Sterilize a small jar so that it is ready to use (see page 14).

2 Drain the anchovies, reserving the oil.

3 Put the anchovies, garlic, shallot and olives in a food processor and, using a pulsating action, blend until the garlic and shallot are finely chopped.

4 Pour 2 tablespoons of the reserved oil through the feed tube and continue blending until a thick paste is formed. Add the lemon juice and parsley and blend again. Season to taste with black pepper.

5 Spoon the mixture into the warmed, sterilized jar, leaving a ½-inch gap at the top. Pour a little extra virgin olive oil over the top to cover the mixture and form a thin layer. Seal immediately and label.

6 Store in the refrigerator up to 2 weeks. Once opened, cover the paste with a layer of oil before returning to the refrigerator.

Chicken Confit

Originating from south-west France, *confit* is one of the oldest methods of preserving poultry. After cooking, the meat is stored in fat, which keeps it moist and tender. The recipe works equally well with duck or chicken.

4 chicken legs
½ cup coarse salt
2 pounds, 4 ounces (4½ cups) duck or goose fat
¼ teaspoon black peppercorns, crushed

½ teaspoon juniper berries, lightly crushed
4 garlic cloves
2 bay leaves, torn in half
4 thyme sprigs

SERVES: 4   PREPARATION TIME: 25 minutes, plus 24 hours curing, 3 to 4 hours cooling and 2 to 3 hours setting   COOKING TIME: 2¾ hours

1 Put the chicken legs in a large, deep dish. Sprinkle the salt over the top of the chicken legs and rub in well. Cover the dish and let cure in the refrigerator 24 hours.

2 When the chicken has cured and you are ready to cook it, rinse well under cold running water and dry with paper towels.

3 Preheat the oven to 300°F.

4 Put the chicken legs in a stoveproof casserole to fit tightly in a single layer. Add the duck or goose fat and heat gently until melted. Make sure that the chicken legs are completely covered in the fat.

5 Add the peppercorns and juniper berries and tuck in the garlic, bay leaves and thyme. Cover the dish.

6 Bake 2½ hours until the meat is very tender. Uncover and let cool 1 hour.

7 Transfer the chicken legs to a large, heatproof dish. Strain the fat and pour it over the chicken legs to cover completely. Leave it 2 to 3 hours until cold.

8 Cover and put in the refrigerator to set. Store in the refrigerator up to 2 weeks.

9 To serve, take the chicken out of the bowl and scrape off most of the fat. Heat a large, heavy skillet and fry the chicken, skin-side-down to begin with, about 10 minutes on each side, until the skin is crisp and golden brown.

Emma's tip The fat can be reused up to three more times to make more *confit* and you can also use the chicken- and garlic-flavored fat for cooking. It is particularly suitable for roasting potatoes and vegetables, but you can also use it to baste other meats and poultry.

Home-cured Chorizo Sausages

It was Matthew "Mash" Chiles' love of European cured meats that inspired him to produce a chorizo sausage using free-range British pork. The Bath Pig Company in Bradford, England, started with experiments using the hot-water-tank cupboard, and is now the largest producer of British charcuterie. This is their original chorizo recipe!

20-inch-long natural sausage casing,
  1¼-inch diameter
1 pound, 5 ounces pork butt, finely chopped
14 ounces pork belly, boned, rind removed and
  finely chopped
1½ ounces (½ cup) Spanish smoked paprika
2 pinches freshly ground black pepper

2 garlic cloves, finely chopped
2½ tablespoons salt, preferably curing salt
  (e.g. Prague powder number 2)
¼ teaspoon acidophilus powder or commercial
  starter culture, if long curing
vinegar, for wiping

MAKES ABOUT: 2 pounds, 4 ounces   PREPARATION TIME: 1 hour, plus 24 to 48 hours chilling and 3 to 4 days or 6 weeks drying

1 Wash the casing under cold running water, ensuring it is clean by turning it inside out and washing again.

2 Put the chopped pork, including its fat, in a large bowl and add the paprika, pepper, garlic and salt. Add acidophilus powder or commercial starter culture if you are experimenting with a long cure but it is not necessary if you wish to make a fresh chorizo for cooking immediately. Add a small splash of water to help bind the mixture, and mix together.

3 Cover the bowl and leave it in the refrigerator 24 to 48 hours for the flavors to develop.

4 Using a sausage pump, fill the sausage casing with the pork mixture. You will find this easier if the casing is wet. Leave a gap at regular intervals and twist to form the sausages.

5 Tie a knot at the end of each sausage link and attach a loop of string for hanging.

6 Let it hang in a well-ventilated, dry, cool, airy place such as a cellar, porch or pantry for 6 weeks for a fully cured sausage or 3 to 4 days if you want to cook them soon. Do not let the sausages touch one another. If there is any danger of flies in your hanging space, cover the sausages in cheesecloth. Use rings inside to keep the cheesecloth away from the sausages so that flies cannot come into contact with them through the cheesecloth.

7 Check regularly for a colored bloom on the outside of the sausages (which can form if the chorizo has been stored in a damp place). A white mold should be expected; a black, blue or yellow mold should not be expected and may not be safe to eat. To help the drying process, wipe down with a cloth dampened in vinegar, which will help stop mold from developing.

Pork Rillettes

Originating from the Loire valley of France, this is a classic way to turn an inexpensive cut of meat into a delicious dish. Serve with crusty French bread as a first course or light meal; Sweet & Sour Cucumber Relish (see page 150) goes well with it.

½ cup coarse salt
2 pounds, 4 ounces pork belly, boned and rind removed
1 pound, 2 ounces pork fat back, chopped
2 garlic cloves

1 Bouquet Garni (see page 196)
¼ teaspoon black peppercorns, crushed
½ teaspoon juniper berries, crushed
1 cup dry white wine
⅓ cup duck or goose fat, if necessary

SERVES: 8 PREPARATION TIME: 45 minutes, plus 24 hours curing, 20 minutes cooling and 2 to 3 hours setting COOKING TIME: 3 to 4 hours

1 Rub the salt into the pork belly well. Put in a dish, cover and leave in the refrigerator 24 hours.

2 Rinse the meat under cold running water and dry with paper towels. Cut the meat into strips about 1-inch thick, and then cut in half. Put the pork belly and fat in an ovenproof casserole dish and mix well.

3 Preheat the oven to 300°F.

4 Tuck the garlic and bouquet garni under the meat. Add the crushed spices and pour in the wine.

5 Cover the dish and bake 3 to 4 hours until the meat is very tender.

6 Discard the bouquet garni. Put the meat in a large strainer over a large bowl and pour over the fat from the casserole. Press the meat lightly with the back of a wooden spoon. Let drain and cool 20 minutes.

7 When the meat is cool enough to handle, remove it from the strainer and, using two forks, pull the meat into shreds. Put the meat in a terrine or ceramic dish.

8 Spoon off most of the fat on top from the bowl and set aside. Pour the juices in the bottom of the bowl over the meat and mix lightly together. Pack the meat into the dish. Pour the spooned-off fat over it to cover the meat; add extra duck or goose fat, if necessary. Cover.

9 Chill the rillettes 2 to 3 hours until the fat has set. Store in the refrigerator up to 2 weeks.

10 To serve, leave at room temperature about 30 minutes. Serve right from the terrine or dish. Once the seal of fat is broken, eat within 3 days.

Emma's tip To vary this recipe, add ½ teaspoon pumpkin pie spice or Chinese five-spice powder.

Cured Leg of Lamb

Curing is still a popular method of preserving in Scandinavia. The conditions must be perfect to prevent the meat from spoiling; start with a small cut of meat first to experiment! The cut of lamb that you use should be cold but don't use lamb that has been frozen because it will absorb more salt than is desired. Traditionally, Cured lamb is served thinly sliced with scrambled eggs or sour cream and crispbreads.

5 pounds cold, lean leg of lamb
18 pounds salt, preferably curing salt (e.g. Prague powder number 2)

vinegar, for wiping

MAKES ABOUT: 5 pounds   PREPARATION TIME: 1 hour, plus 3 days curing and 4 months maturing

1 Squeeze the meat to remove as much blood as possible. Work from the top end and repeat several times. Remove any surplus fat and pieces of meat that hang from the leg. Wash the meat under cold running water and dry well on paper towels.

2 Cover the bottom of a large dish with about 1 inch of the salt. Add the meat and rub more salt over the leg until it is well covered, massaging into the cuts and crevices. Cover with a mesh food cover and put in a cool place at a temperature of 39 to 41°F. Leave it 3 days, turning and moving the leg every day, until the meat gives off a clear or pink liquid. Add extra salt if necessary so that the meat is always covered.

3 When the meat has cured, rinse well under cold running water and pat dry with paper towels.

4 Attach a loop of string for hanging. If there is any danger of flies in your hanging place, cover the meat in cheesecloth. Use rings inside to keep the cheesecloth away from the meat so that flies cannot come into contact with the meat through the cheesecloth.

5 Let it hang in a well-ventilated, dry, cool, airy place such as a cellar, porch or pantry at a temperature of 41 to 50°F for about 4 months. The leg should have a gray surface, be completely dry, firm to the touch but still have some give when pressed with the thumb. Check regularly for a colored bloom on the outside. A white mold should be expected; a black, blue or yellow mold should not be expected and may not be safe to eat. To help the drying process, wipe it down with a cloth dampened in vinegar, which will help stop mold from developing. If kept dry, in air and away from flies, the lamb can last up to a year. It will become drier and saltier over time.

Index

About the Author

Emma Macdonald, a trained chef, founded The Bay Tree Food Co. from her mother's kitchen table. Selling into Waitrose and multinational stores, as well as independent delis across the UK, The Bay Tree is now a well-known and popular quality brand producer of sauces, relishes, jams, dressings and chutneys in the UK. Emma lives in the West Country with her husband and three sons and is also the author of *Home Deli Recipes*.

Acknowledgements

To all those who have once again toiled blood, sweat and tears to help me in putting together this book, it is not without huge thanks. Thanks also to all those who have had to put up with me whilst I have been working on this book; without you all it would not have been possible. I hope it will be enjoyed by many in the quest for the perfect preserve!

NOURISH
EAT WELL, LIVE WELL

We hope you've enjoyed this Nourish book. Here at Nourish we're all about wellbeing through food and drink – irresistible dishes with a serious good-for-you factor. If you want to eat and drink delicious things that set you up for the day, suit any special diets, keep you healthy and make the most of what you can afford, we've got some great ideas to share with you. Come over to our blog for wholesome recipes and fresh inspiration – nourishbooks.com.